NOTTINGHAM

Edited by Chris Hallam

First published in Great Britain in 2003 by
YOUNG WRITERS
Remus House,
Coltsfoot Drive,
Peterborough, PE2 9JX
Telephone (01733) 890066

SB ISBN 1 84460 288 5

FOREWORD

Young Writers was established in 1991 as a foundation for promoting the reading and writing of poetry amongst children and young adults. Today it continues this quest and proceeds to nurture and guide the writing talents of today's youth.

From this year's competition Young Writers is proud to present a showcase of the best poetic talent from across the UK. Each hand-picked poem has been carefully chosen from over 66,000 'Hullabaloo!' entries to be published in this, our eleventh primary school series.

This year in particular we have been wholeheartedly impressed with the quality of entries received. The thought, effort, imagination and hard work put into each poem impressed us all and once again the task of editing was a difficult but enjoyable experience.

We hope you are as pleased as we are with the final selection and that you and your family will continue to be entertained with *Hullabaloo! Nottingham* for many years to come.

CONTENTS

Melanie Nice (10)	21
Amie Godber (9)	21
Rebecca Kellam (10)	22
Lewis Archer (10)	22
Kaya Hutton (9)	23
Danielle Oliver (9)	23
Michael O'Hare (11)	24
Shannon Brown (10)	24
Yasmin Sims (11)	25
Cara Holmes (11)	25
Victoria Fowler (11)	26
Matthew Stott (10)	26
Natalie Kirk (11)	27
Jordan Watson (10)	27
Rae Swift (10)	28
Lucie Parkes (10)	28
Laura Gilliver (10)	29
Lauren Godfrey (9)	30
Callum Mortimer (9)	31
Emma Staples (10)	31
Ellechia Cole (10)	32
Tesfaye Bennett (9)	33
Alice Logan (11)	34
Justine Sharp (9)	34
Neil Walker (11)	35
Rhian Raynor (11)	35
Michael Tyers (10)	36
Harry White (10)	36
Kim Oliver (11)	37
Liam Jayes (11)	37
Tafari Bennett (11)	38
Daniel Sweet (10)	38
Kathryn Dennis (11)	39

Chetwynd Road Primary School

Isabel Marriott (8)	40
William Stevenson (8)	40
Leah Stone (8)	41

Emma Marshall (8)	42
Kieran Halpin (8)	42
Alexandra Springhall (8)	43
Joel Patchitt (7)	44
Ben Wormald (7)	44
Laurence Williamson (7)	45
Chelsea Grace (7)	46
Matthew Peall (7)	47
Tony Grimes (7)	47
Emily Dainty (8)	48
Ashley Hall (8)	49
Emily Lupino-Poole (7)	49
Katie Morrice (7)	50
Harvey Perttola (7)	51
Callum Henderson (8)	52
Kyle Thompson (8)	52
Sam Mansfield (7)	53
Christopher Waddington (9)	53
Sarah Buckley (8)	54
Charlotte Pick (7)	55
Ahranee Canden (8)	56
Thomas Corcoran (8)	56
Nila Rochester (9)	57
Christopher Gray (9)	57
Charlotte Hughes (9)	58
Samuel Hands (8)	58
Elizabeth Jones (9)	59
Lydia Youle (8)	59
Sophie Naylor (8)	60
Ross Osborne (9)	60
Charlotte Brick (9)	61
Zoe Cook (8)	61
Josh Knight (9)	62

Cloudside Junior School

Stephanie Blanco (10)	63
Joseph Oldham (11)	63
Jared Pointer (11)	64

Jade Nicholson (10)	83
Abigail O'Loughlin (7) & Charlotte Harris (8)	84
Honor Duff (10)	84
Kariss Miles (10)	85
Clare Billington (9)	86
Louise Brace (9)	86
Rose Heppell (10)	87
Lucy Dinsdale (9)	87
Holly Jennings (10)	88
Stephen Allison (11)	88
Kimberley Squires (10)	89
Johnathon Slack (9)	90
Daniel Brookes (10)	91
Nicola Bilbie (10)	92
Danielle Nelson (9)	93
Jessica Bavin (11)	93
Gemma France (10)	94
Gary Beach (10)	94
Sophie Edmonds (10)	95
Adam Palmer (11)	95
Laura Ames (11)	96
Gemma Ames (11)	96
Dameon Taylor (10)	97
Leanne Smith (10)	97
Leigh Feranti (11)	98
Victoria Block (11)	98
Vikki Brooks & Chloe Featherstone (7)	99
Nichol Oak-Smith (8)	100
Ashley Brooks (10) & Shannon Bailey (11)	101

Firbeck Primary School

Demi Salt (9)	101
Melike Berker (10)	102
Christian Voce (9)	103
Michael Charles (9)	104
Gary Charles (11)	104
Reema Khalid (10)	105
Chloe Robinson (9)	105

Nicholas Powell (9)	125
Anna Bradley (9)	126
George Farraj (9)	126
Thomas Vickerstaff (10)	127
Jack Dickie (10)	128
Charlie Scott (10)	129
Charles Shortland (11)	129
Ross Whiting (10)	130
Ellika Larsson (10)	131
Alex Brown (10)	131
Elizabeth Harper (10)	132
Samuel Robinson (10)	132
Sam Buxton (10)	133
Alexandra Hearth (10)	134
Jonathan Lister (10)	135
Ian Welch (10)	136

Keyworth Primary & Nursery School

Liam Carroll (8)	136
Ethan Moult (7)	137
Hannah Reilly (9)	137
Sarah Robins (9)	138
Jacob Sjenitzer (7)	138
Evie Clegg (7)	139
Ellie Snooks (8)	139
Thomas Burrows (7)	140
Luke Woolley (8)	141
Edward Welham (7)	141

Nottingham Girls' High School

Katie Taylor (11)	142
Emily Oliver (10)	143
Jess Engler (10)	144
Rebecca Donaldson (10)	145
Daisy Gudmunsen (11)	145
Rachel Kenny (11)	146
Kate Selwyn (10)	146
Elly Gladman (10)	147

Anna Redgate (11)   148
Nidhi Sahdev (11)   149
Rebecca Brown (10)   150
Sophia Ali (11)   150
Sophie Reeve (10)   151
Rosie Lenaghan (10)   151
Jessica Moses (11)   152
Megan Holmes (10)   152
Ebele Egbuna-Ruiz (11)   153
Abigail Packham (11)   153
Sonali Chandi (10)   154
Georgina Robertson (10)   154
Jasmin Evans (10)   155
Annie Hud (10)   156
Helen Poulson (11)   157
Catherine Rhodes-Jones (10)   157
Jessica Crooks (10)   158
Alice Conlin (10)   158

Robin Hood Junior School
Stacie Butler (10)   159
Daniel Marshall (11)   159
Kimberley Brown (10)   160
Sam Bramley (10)   160
Natalie Garner (11)   161
Steven Higgins (11)   161
Zoë-Maria Wright (11)   162
Ashley Warsop (11)   162
Mark Thornton (11)   163
Chantelle Brown (10)   163
Katie Ley (10)   164
Sean Duryea (10)   164
Nathan Watson (10)   165
Sadie Duryea (10)   165
Jemma Ward (11)   166
Rhys Donaghy (11)   166
Ryan Bush (10)   167
Amanda Broughton (11)   167

St Edmund Campion RC Primary School

Stanstead Primary School

Katie Dickinson (9)	203
Thomas Stovell & Corey McGhee (8)	203
Thomas Savage & Jay Jackson (9)	204
Jessica Brazener (8)	204
Aiesha McLaren (9)	205
Joshua O'Sullivan (9)	205
Louise Banister (8)	206
Sophie Liddiard (9)	206
Nicky Rood (9)	207
Kieran Booth (9)	207
Justin Scothern (10)	208
Liam Bostock (9)	208
Liam Baker (9)	209
Ricky Wootton (10)	209
Chris Wilson (9)	209
Thomas Crampton (9)	210
Danny Wheeler (10)	210
Luke Bass (9)	211
Rachel Reid (9)	211

The Poems

FOOTBALL

I love playing football
But people say I can't play
But why can't I play?
Is it because I'm rubbish?

I'd love to play football
People say I'm not allowed
But why can't I play?
Is it that they don't like me?

I'd still love to play football
I really wish I could
Oh why can't I play?
Maybe because I'm a girl!

Kate Williamson (9)
Attenborough Preparatory School

MY BROTHER!

My brother is a pest
He always makes a mess!
He is a nuisance to me
And to the rest I see!

He's always throwing toys about
And I have to pick them up!
He whinges when he goes to bed
And always wakes me up!

Megan McCausland (7)
Attenborough Preparatory School

COLOURS

Red, green, yellow and blue
Colours are everywhere
Grey, black, white as well
Colours are everywhere
On the roof
On the floor
On the wall
On the door
Violet, purple, pink as well
Colours are everywhere
Leaves are green
Teddies can be any colour
Colours are everywhere
Colours are in the school
Colours are in the house
On the crayons
In the sky
Colours are everywhere
Brown, silver, gold as well
Colours are everywhere!

Charlie Howarth (8)
Attenborough Preparatory School

MY CAT

My cat Frankie
Always thanks me
For giving her a bowl of food
Howling crossly
Crying 'Possibly?
Could I have my tea today?'

Amelia Greatorex (10)
Attenborough Preparatory School

THE RACE

When I start a race
I know I can win with my pace.
Suddenly a cheer starts from the stand
I shoot from the line like a rubber band.
I beat number one, number two and number four.
And in my ear I can hear the roar
Of an excited crowd.

The wind rushes past
As I go fast
With my heart pumping
Can't wait for my jumping.
My tired feet pound the ground
I can't hear a sound
As I cross the line
        I've won!

Joe Langford (9)
Attenborough Preparatory School

MY LITTLE BROTHER

My little brother is such a pest
He picks my things up and makes a mess
He throws them about making me mad
'Little brother don't do that you'll wake up Dad!'

Of course you should have known he did not listen!
He made such a noise that Dad woke up on a mission
He started shouting, so I said:
'Little brother, just go back to bed!'

Samuel Gauntley (8)
Attenborough Preparatory School

CRICKET

On a gleaming afternoon
in the cricket ground
I was sitting back with my eyes closed
Listening to the smooth leather ball hitting the willow bat,
As the crowd cheered or clapped their hands,
When suddenly there was a change in the wind,
The crowd roared with delight for the team had won,
The peace was surely over everybody moved around
Now I can go home and have a think:

Of the clicking noise of the ball hitting the bat,
The crowd cheering and clapping,
The odd appeal of a wicket
And of course the feeling of being at the game.

Adam Pringle (9)
Attenborough Preparatory School

PLANES

Jets fly fast
Always with a blast
Whizzing through the air
With not a minute to spare.
The Red Arrows ahead
With nothing to dread
They have lots of speed that they don't even need
Planes are the best, so leave the rest
Planes are cool
I wish they had them in school.

Alex Reeder (9)
Attenborough Preparatory School

WAVES

Waves are exciting
They can be massive and small
Especially the ones that *crash* on the shore.

The waves that are small and trickle on the sand
Are boring me more and more . . .

The surfers are surfing on gigantic waves
Splashing small boats and distracting people from their sleep.

I love the sound of the waves splashing on the shore
But having to wait for an ice cream is boring me more and more . . .

Alex Jameson (9)
Attenborough Preparatory School

THE GREAT WALL OF CHINA

The Great Wall of China
The only man-made structure seen from space.
Endless, twisty and slithery,
Like a giant sea monster slithering through the hills.
Like a monstrous snake weaving over hills.
I feel minuscule and microscopic
Like a tiny garden spider next to a huge building.
The Great Wall of China
Makes me wonder what people do to stop others.

Priyan Rayatt (11)
Attenborough Preparatory School

STUNTMAN

It's five minutes till the jump
If he fails he would not get just a lump.
The amazing stuntman steps in the car
And has a little chocolate bar.
He starts the V16 engine with a roar
Shaking to the core.

He puts the pedal to the floor
Always checking to lock the door.
The ramp was coming to him fast
He remembered dreams in the past.
But suddenly the axle broke
He ran all out of hope.
He was flying through the air
Spinning without a care.

The crowd holds its breath
As he plunges to his death
But wait, they gasp
Out of the burning wreckage and shattered
Glass he came,
And with a stumble put his arms up to the cheering crowd.
The famous stuntman lives again.

Oliver Lloyd (10)
Attenborough Preparatory School

WINTER'S HERE

Snow is falling all around
Touching me
And the ground.
The snow is like a blanket
Fallen from the sky in the dark night.
Morning comes
A silent, peaceful world.
Trees standing tall,
Leaves frozen stiff
Against the golden sky
Of a misty morning.

Ben Mason (10)
Attenborough Preparatory School

TELEVISION

Watching TV is the life for me!
There's always something to watch,
Cartoons . . .
Football . . .
The lot!
Sitting on the edge of my chair,
Hypnotised.
Mum says I watch too much TV
Never!
Because it's the life for me.

Joseph Williamson (11)
Attenborough Preparatory School

DETENTION

Dong! Dong! Dong! Dong!
The school bell's ringing like a gong
But I know that I have to stay
Because I've been given detention for the day.
I got it this morning just before school
And our mean old teacher, Mr Ghoul
Said that I came in late for maths
And that I had to stay in after class.
I think my mum will be cross with me
And I'll be in bed without my tea.
But what is this, can it be?
Is that really what I see?
I stared at the window that was agape
The perfect way to make my escape.
The hairs on my neck stood up straight
I could get home for tea, it wasn't too late.
I ran like an athlete, I felt so free!
'I'm out of school!' I shouted with glee.
I ran like lightning from the road
Past lorries carrying their heavy loads.
I had to get home, there was so much to do,
I was just in time for dinner too!

Joe Goring (10)
Attenborough Preparatory School

THE BALLET LESSON

On the tip of my toes,
As we stand straight in our rows,
With elegance and beauty,
Performing sautées and jumps.
My head held high and my tummy pulled in,
Ready to embark on a pirouette spin.
As I step to the barre doing pliés and points,
And exercising to bend and extend my flexible joints.
Pas de chat, which is the step of a cat,
Is lively and energetic like catching a rat!
I stand like a swan - graceful, sleek and tall,
I prepare myself for the most beautiful ballet position of all!
Arms extended, like a bird in flight,
As I stretch my legs and pose my arms with all my might.
There is no comparison, this is undoubtedly the best,
The perfectly balanced, graceful curve of the arabesque!

Flavia Percox (10)
Attenborough Preparatory School

FAMILY'S GONE MAD

Mummy's dying,
Baby's crying,
Daddy's running downstairs,
Grandma is growing green hair,
Grandad has gone to the pub to drink one or two.

Katie Law (10)
Cantrell Primary School

MY FAMILY'S POEM

Everyone has a family
They're all over the world
Australia or Jamaica
Britain or Ireland.
In families there are
Grans and Grandpas,
And a Mum and a Dad.
Aunties and Uncles, Cousins.
We definitely have families
Old, young or even new!
They will always love you.
Brothers, Sisters,
Baby brothers and sisters.
Mum stepsister wearing funny frocks
Dad silly brother's wearing shorts in winter.
Family are from Asia and Finland
China or America.
They're all very funny
And never ever boring.
A very friendly family
Non unfriendly
Stepbrothers, stepsisters
Stepmum, stepdads,
Stepgran and stepgrampas
Stepaunties and stepuncles
It doesn't really matter
But they're all our family!

Kirstie Putt (9)
Cantrell Primary School

MORNING MADNESS

Baby brother's moved it
Baby sister's gone, cousin can't find it
Don't turn the light on
Shouting up the apples and pears
Dad stamping down the stairs
Friends knocking on the door
What are you waiting for?
Pour out the cereal
No time Muriel.
We need to get to school
Mum stay cool
Get out the door
Wait for the bus
No time to fuss
Wait for my friend
What . . . it's the weekend!

Conor Jackson (9)
Cantrell Primary School

BALLOON

Up in the air like a rising sun
Floating and dancing about like a dancer.
Red, yellow, green and blue,
All the colours of the rainbow I can be.
Buy me, sell me,
At a fair or at a dance.
Blow me up and I will rise
Buy me in bags of ten or buy me on my own.

Nicholas Brown (11)
Cantrell Primary School

SWEETS AND TREATS

In my house I have a cupboard
That is full of delicious sweets
Fizzy sweets
Big sweets
Chocolate and treats
Every day, every night
I have some sweets and treats.
Eating them in funny ways, weird ways too.
I love sweets, I love treats
It's treats and sweets all day long like
Long sweets
Short sweets
Square sweets
Round sweets too.
    I . . . love . . . sweets!

Charlotte Willey (9)
Cantrell Primary School

SKATEBOARD

Skateboard
Skateboard
Fly down the road
Skateboard
Skateboard
Don't forget the Green Cross Code!
Skateboard
Skateboard
It is so great
Skateboard
Skateboard
It becomes your mate.

Jake Day (11)
Cantrell Primary School

LIFE IN THE WOODS

You go to the woods
all day and all night
any year, any month
or any time.

You will see the animals
once or twice
they're very cute
but I like the mice.

There are fish and crocodiles
Elephants and ants
We all like animals
So give them a chance.

A chance to live
Under trees in the shade
A chance to live in the sun
To play.

But you'll see the animals if you . . .

Go to the woods all day
and all night
any year, any month
or any time.

Gemma Tuckwood (10)
Cantrell Primary School

MY FAMILY POEM

My family is very big
There's nannas, grandads,
Mums and dads
Brothers and sisters
Uncles and aunties
And lots of other relations.
We have family pets
Food and sweets
And photos of the olden days.

Thursday is Grandparents' Day
When we visit we eat them out of house and home.
In the summer
We take trips to the seaside
To Ingoldmells and Skeggy.
We also go swimming, picnicing and
Trips to the zoo.
But in the winter
We stay indoors or go
For a walk in the snow.

After Christmas on New Year's Eve
We have fun and games till midnight.
But in the morning we are tired and lazy
In bed till dinner.
But on birthdays, we are excited and
Full of laughter.
But everyone is a year older.

Amelia Donnelly (10)
Cantrell Primary School

SPORTS

Football is a really good game,
But all the others are the same.
Cricket is when you hit it,
And then you hit the wicket.
Tennis you play when you're watching
Dennis the Menace.
The javelin who hit someone with a grin,
You play with a basketball
Then you fall.
Baseball you can play while you are small,
Hockey was played by the Rockies,
But the last one that I love
Most of all
Is the volleyball.
You hit it over the fence,
Then you say, 'Where's the defence?'
You jump, you run, you kick
But you also light a candlestick.

Haydn Fisher (10)
Cantrell Primary School

PLAY TIME

Play time is cool
When we're at school
The school bell rings
Dill a ling ling
We pick up our coats
And put them in the cloakroom
Ready for lesson time.

Kirsty Thomas (10)
Cantrell Primary School

FOOTBALL

Running, running towards the goal,
Trying to outskill Andy Cole.

Roy Keane is always mean,
He only plays with his team.

If you don't score!
The crowds won't roar.

I support Liverpool,.
They're the best,
Better than all the rest.

The big match is here,
Man U v Liverpool,
I wonder who is going to win.

After ninety minutes,
The whistle has gone,
And a two - nil easy victory to Liverpool.

Ben Cordon (10)
Cantrell Primary School

MOON

Moon, moon, wonderful moon
You're so bright, you light up my room.
You come down right to the ground
Moon, moon, wonderful moon.
Wonderful moon, talk to me
For evermore you will be with me.

Stacey Evans (10)
Cantrell Primary School

HOBBIES ARE GREAT

Hobbies are fun
Hobbies are great
You can do them in rain or sun
You can do them with a mate.
Football's for boys
Dancing's for girls
Some hobbies are quiet
And some hobbies make noise
You can do them in a field
Or do them in a hall.
For some you use your body
For some you use a ball
Boys like running
Girls like singing
And everyone loves swimming.
There are different hobbies around the world
I love hobbies
Hobbies are great.

Hannah Mann (10)
Cantrell Primary School

HALLOWE'EN

Ghosts and goblins walk the street
Witches and wizards are the people you meet.
Pumpkins in windows with candles aglow
Spiders in webs that glow like snow.
Devils with horns and long spiky sticks,
But beware of the spikes that come out of their lips.

Shane Hinton (11)
Cantrell Primary School

SUMMER

People go to swim in outdoor pools
Spring has ended, summer is here
Animals start to play
Grass starts to grow again
Lambs grow up and sheep die
Children enjoy the holidays
Birds start to chirp
People take their children out
Trees grow leaves
Farm animals are allowed outside
The sun comes out
Children start to play outside
Flowers grow tall and pretty
People go on holiday
And spend more time outside
School has ended for the summer
Friends from other schools meet to play games.

Adam Gilson (9)
Cantrell Primary School

STARS

Stars, stars wonderful stars
You come out at night,
All I see is you the most at night,
But I can't wait till tomorrow night.
I'll see you once again
You'll be no bigger or no smaller.

Lucinda Harding (10)
Cantrell Primary School

IN A BIG WOODEN BOX . . .

In a big wooden box . . .
I saw a big furry fox.
I saw a baby chick
That went click.
Then I saw a mouse
In a very little house.
An old grandfather clock
That went tick-tock.
An old ice cream cone
A broken phone.
A dog with a collar
Then the next thing you know a cat
A dollar
A skeleton on chains
A horse on reins
My sister's old coat
Sailing on a boat
My dad going mad
Oh I wish I had
The dog barking like mad
Me going bad doggy, bad.

Tiffany Colagiovanni (10)
Cantrell Primary School

ANIMALS

Running, jumping, leaping, walking,
Horses do all this, they just need to start talking.

Pets, pets, pets, pets,
Stop catching them in nets.

Cats, cats, cats, cats,
Like lovely, warm, soft mats.

Dogs, rabbits, chimps, birds,
Lots of animals come in herds.

Dolphins, dolphins, dolphins, dolphins
Stop treating them like old things.

'Mum, let me have a chimp,'
'No because lots of them are limp.'

Dogs, dogs, dogs, dogs,
Some are friends with frogs.

Crabs, mice, swans, hens,
All bunch up in one big den.

Bugs, bugs, bugs, bugs,
'Look! One's in my mug.'

Deer, deer, deer, deer,
Most of them are afraid of bears.

Kirsty Galloway (10)
Cantrell Primary School

MY DOG

My dog is always fun, well most of the time anyway.
The garden is his favourite place, where he likes to play.
I like him because he is very furry
And for a dog he is quite worthy.
My dog likes to laze about,
He sleeps on the sofa
Which makes my mum shout.
We like to play tug a war
And when we come in from the garden
There's always muddy footprints on the floor.
We both like watching football
While eating breakfast cereal.
My dog hates baths
And when he jumps out it makes me laugh.
My dog hates cats.
My mum put him on a terrible diet
Because he was getting fat!
I love my dog I will never swap him,
I'll keep my word
Forever I promise.

Melanie Nice (10)
Cantrell Primary School

THE BLAZING SUN

The blazing sun comes out to play, it is a beautiful day.
The sun is like a warm fire like everyone wants to desire.
The powerful sun likes the sky and when people say bye.
The roasting sun likes to play when it says hello to you all day long.
The sun is like a hot boiling fire which you can sit near with a desire.
The sun shines bright like a light.

Amie Godber (9)
Cantrell Primary School

FRIENDS

Friends are caring,
Friends are cool,
Friends are wicked,
You meet most of them at school.

Friends are always there for you,
Whether you're sad or happy,
They're always there to talk,
To make you feel so jolly.

You go out onto the playground,
They're all a different type,
One funny, one bright, one who cares for you
And one who gives you a fright.

No matter what they look like,
No matter what they do,
Friends are always going to be there for me and you!

Rebecca Kellam (10)
Cantrell Primary School

FOOTBALL

Football, football
Is so cool
Cantrell whoops
Every school.
Get that ball
Make it yours
Score a goal
Then you'll hear
A great applause.

Lewis Archer (10)
Cantrell Primary School

FRIENDS

Friends are always there for you
Whenever you are feeling blue
Friends are always very caring
Friends are always kind and sharing
You love to talk and sing and play
You see them almost every day
Friends are very, very cool
You always meet up on the way to school.
Friends are there when something's wrong,
They cheer you up with your fave song.
You like it when they come round for tea
You nearly always watch TV.
You always meet at the weekend
Everybody needs a *friend!*

Kaya Hutton *(9)*
Cantrell Primary School

FRIENDS

Leave your supper and leave your sleep
And join your fellows out on the street.
Your friends are the best, yes most of all,
Give your friends a loud big call.

Knock on the door it's time to play
It is time to go to the park today.
It's getting late, it's time to go in,
We will be there in a gip and a spin.

It's the end of Saturday,
So we can play out again on Sunday.

Danielle Oliver *(9)*
Cantrell Primary School

THE TEACHER'S DAY

On Monday morning bright and shine,
The teacher settles down.
She gets up, walks about,
Saying finally some sunshine.

> Quick, quick, kick that ball
> Drive the teacher up the wall.
> Quick, quick, ring that bell,
> Drive the teacher into Hell.

Today it is science, English and maths,
She hates them all because of the class.
Class 4P the worst class ever,
She feels like a piece of leather.

> Quick, quick, kick that ball
> Drive the teacher up the wall.
> Quick, quick, ring that bell
> Drive the teacher into Hell.

Michael O'Hare (11)
Cantrell Primary School

THE SUN

T he sun is cool because it's hot
H olidays we go when it gets hot
E gypt I love that staying in a caravan

S ummer, summer, it's all great, can't wait
   until next year
U nder the sun we get a suntan
N ever forget to put your suncream on
   because you will get burnt!

Shannon Brown (10)
Cantrell Primary School

SCHOOL DINNERS

School dinners taste so sick,
They sure do get on my wick.
Their deadly smell,
Makes me feel funny
As it pops up
Out of my tummy.

School dinners taste so sick,
They sure do get on my wick.
The mushy peas
Are more like bogies.
With black sausage rolls
And rock hard cookies.

School dinners taste so sick,
They sure do get on my wick.
Sneak them in the bin,
Flush 'em down the toilet.
Get rid of them somehow,
Cos your appetite gets spoilt!

Yasmin Sims (11)
Cantrell Primary School

MY HOMEWORK

My dog ate my homework,
I'll bring my homework in tomorrow.
My mum flushed it down the toilet Miss,
I'll bring a new piece in tomorrow Miss.
I started to eat it, I'll bring it in tomorrow Miss.
Miss, I've brought it in today.

Cara Holmes (11)
Cantrell Primary School

It's Cool To Be In School!

It's cool to be in class
And I like maths.
So I enjoy going to the swimming baths
So it's cool to be in class.

It's cool to be in school
You should like at least one subject
It should be maths.

It's cool to be in class,
I would like to pass
The Year 6 big tests
Which are called the SATs.

It's cool to be in school
You should like at least one subject
It should be maths.

It's cool to be in school!

Victoria Fowler (11)
Cantrell Primary School

Wet Play Time

I've always hated wet play time
When the clouds burst and let out the rain
We all have to stay in school
And I'm in a daydream all the time.

I've always hated wet play time
Until that one the other day
We all had a big pen fight
And teacher gave us detention.

Matthew Stott (10)
Cantrell Primary School

FAMILY POEM

Mum is great and Dad is cool
Grandad's in the pub having one or two
Mammas are in the house being very silly.

Sophie is at school trying her best at all the work
Brandon is in the house being very sleepy
Abbie is at school playing and playing all day long.

Mum is great and Dad is cool
Grandad's in the pub having one or two
Mammas are in the house being very silly.

Blue, red, orange, green, yellow and all different colours
Rockets are great
There is lots of food and drinks
I love it.

Natalie Kirk (11)
Cantrell Primary School

A SUNNY DAY

It is a sunny day and the sun comes up.
The sun is as bright as a big fire.
The sun is as hot as a fireball.
It is burning away as a fire.

People run out to play on the beach
But are too hot
So they jump in the water to play in.

After the sun went down everybody said
We will hope for a hot bright day like today.

Jordan Watson (10)
Cantrell Primary School

WINTER HAIKU!

December
Shiny snow that's white
Weather freezing cold and wet
The long nights are dark.

January
Snow not so often
Raining nearly every day
Ice makes fingers glow.

February
Very cold and damp
Chilly at night, nose turns red
Slippery pavements.

Rae Swift (10)
Cantrell Primary School

WEATHER CRASH

Beautiful sun in the summer
As hot as a raging fire.

Storm swirling from the sky
When it goes we say goodbye.

When it snows it's so much fun
We play with snowballs all through the day.

We love weather, we do.

   Crash
   Crash
   Crash

All through the day.

Lucie Parkes (10)
Cantrell Primary School

THE STORMY NIGHT

A fisherman's boat was hauled out of the harbour
On a storm-raising night.

Three men went to catch fish with fright.
When they sailed further into the sea,
The boat disappeared, the men too, all three.

The waves were higher than ever,
I bet they wished they never came out, never!

The lighthouse beamed with lights,
As the fishermen's boat was sinking.

All because of the storm-raising night,
And they came with fright.

To catch fish for their village,
And put their lives at risk.

When some people searched for clues,
Floating in the sea was a photo of the men, all happy.
Jolly as can be.

Then out of the blue a voice shouted,
'Help, please anybody help!'
Said one voice then another and another.

The men were all rescued,
The sea did do something right,
It also made them sink and pushed them to shore.

Because of the storm-raising night
When they went out in fright
To catch fish on that storm-raising night.

Laura Gilliver (10)
Cantrell Primary School

THE POWERFUL SUN

The sun shoots up
Then pops out to rise
It is like a strong cup
Out it comes with a surprise.

There was never a breeze,
It was not cold,
You would never freeze,
There was never mould.

It springs across the trees
It is a jumping frog,
Which has risen upon the log,
There's no fleece - (in these trees).

The sun's turned pink,
With a bashing blink,
What's the inch,
There's no flinch.

It became dark
Out came the arc
The sunset,
I'll give you three dollars,
I bet.

Lauren Godfrey (9)
Cantrell Primary School

STORMY WEATHER

The waves were crashing against the boats,
The lightning was crashing down powerfully
It was a storm forming.

The rain was diving into the sea like meteorites,
The thunder was rumbling like an earthquake,
The black clouds were erupting volcanoes,
The waves were crushing the boats.

A boat was flooding with water,
When lightning struck the mast.
Waves the size of Scotland went over
The boat and crushed it.

Callum Mortimer (9)
Cantrell Primary School

SUN & WARMTH

The sun was as warm as a hot fire,
The sea was as cool as cold water,
The sand was like the breeze that was cool and slow,
The sky was as blue as the lovely sea.

The sunrays were yellow sweets,
The sea was cool swirls,
The sand was as soft as a cuddly bear,
The sky was as clear as a diamond.

The sun was as red as a devil,
The sea was as smooth as a marble,
The sand was as straight as a pole.

Emma Staples (10)
Cantrell Primary School

THE WEATHER

The wind, the rain, the snow, the sun,
Whatever the weather, you can always have fun.

The wind is blowing in my hair
The wind is flying through the air.
The wind is fun, the wind is great, all day and night.
The wind is rough, the wind can go
      Crash, bash and bang.

The wind can blow things down which
will make you want to frown.

The rain can make you sad
When it is very bad.
I am always very glad when it is not so very bad.
Rain helps with many things like making things grow
Year after year and making sure the rivers never disappear.

Snow makes me freeze like ice
On a cold winter's night.
It can be fun when you slip on your bum.
You can skate on ice, sledge on the snow,
You can have lots of fun to and fro in the snow.

The sun is fun, you can grow flowers in the sun.
Feel the warmth on your skin.
Makes you happy when things are looking grim.

Whatever the weather you can always have fun
Even when it is pretty glum.

Ellechia Cole (10)
Cantrell Primary School

THE WEATHER

The sun is a steamed coal fire,
The sun is a fire star
But the sun is a liar
The sun is as bright as the stars
That shine in the night sky,
The sun is as hot as a desert
And is hot as a burning radiator
I lay down and stare at the sun
The bright, bright sun.

It is raining very fast,
Quickly everyone, inside.
It's chucking it down with rain,
Everyone has their wellies on if they're out
If they're inside they're playing a certain game.

In the snow everyone's nice and warm
Wrapped up in scarves, gloves, hats and coats.
The snow is like ice from a freezer,
Falling from the sky
Everybody's playing in the snow,
Snowballs flying in the air
The snow is wonderful but is very cold.

Tesfaye Bennett (9)
Cantrell Primary School

HOMEWORK!

'Where's your homework?'
'Dog chewed it up Sir.'
'Where's your homework?'
'Alien took it, Sir.'
'Where's your homework?'
'Sent it to Spain, Sir.'
'Where's your homework?'
'Flushed it down the loo, Sir.'
'Where's your homework?'
'Painted a portrait on it, Sir.'
'Where's your homework?'
'Turned it into a plane, Sir.'
'Where's your homework?'
'Turned it into Christmas present wrapping, Sir.'
'Where's your homework?'
'OK I didn't do it!'

Alice Logan (11)
Cantrell Primary School

ON A COLD, CLOUDY, CHILLY DAY

On a cold, cloudy, chilly day,
All the children went to play,
On a cold, cloudy, chilly day.
All the children say, 'Why do we have to run away?'
On a cold, cloudy, chilly day.
All the people jumped in the hay,
On a cold, cloudy, chilly day.
All the adults love May
On a cold, cloudy, chilly day.
All the children play with clay,
On a cold, cloudy, chilly day.

Justine Sharp (9)
Cantrell Primary School

SPELLING ACROSTIC

S   pelling all different words like answer or
    explosion
P   ractising your spellings for the spelling test
E   asy, medium or hard that is how you think they are
L   earning all new words
L   earning them every day of the week
I   n the test everyone's quiet
N   ow I'm in my house learning my spellings
G   etting three tens out of ten, three weeks in a row
    you get a week *off!*

Neil Walker (11)
Cantrell Primary School

SCHOOL DINNERS

I shall tell you what I found out yesterday.
Excuse me I need right of way.
I asked a school dinnerlady and
She said:
'Spaghetti is chunky pieces of hair,
Salads are *poisonous* fruits from the rainforest.
Vegetables are painted pieces of railings.
Mushy peas are bogies.
Chips are twigs
And worst of all is that,
Jelly with cream is really
Red slime and frog larvae.'
So please whatever you do don't have
            School Dinners.

Rhian Raynor (11)
Cantrell Primary School

MY TEACHER IS AN ALIEN

My teacher is an alien
He comes from outer space
He stops every fight
And writes at the speed of light.

He knows every equation
And knows everything else
He has radar vision
And knows his long division.

His name is Mr Know It All
He thinks he is the best
Then I came and beat him
At the spelling test.

Michael Tyers (10)
Cantrell Primary School

ALIEN IN DETENTION

An alien got detention
He didn't know what it meant
He wasn't paying attention
Because he was mean.

When he got in there
He was moaning and groaning.
Always he would stare
And he was called Zool Branning.

When he got out he was so happy
He said '*Erty gfds lalien*'
But he was so slappy
Because he was an alien.

Harry White (10)
Cantrell Primary School

SICK AT HOME

Oh Miss I'm sick
Please don't take the mick.
Oh darling, we must phone home
And *please do not moan.*

I fell asleep on the couch
Oh please do not crouch.
Stay here till I come back
OK my mum while you're gone
I'll take a nap.

Mum's gone, I have the house
I will set free the mouse.
Turn on the disco lights, CD player
At least I'm not doing boring *Dare*
The party's done, go mouse, Mum's come!

Kim Oliver (11)
Cantrell Primary School

THE DRAGON WHO VISITED OUR SCHOOL

When the dragon came to visit our school
He had a swim in the pool
We all thought it was cool
When he came to visit our school.

He took a look around
And he found
A pound
On the school ground
When the dragon came to visit our school.

Liam Jayes (11)
Cantrell Primary School

BRUMFRO

Once there was a boy called bullying Jim
Who loved motorbikes.
Here's a rap about him.
Brum brum down the street
He gets off his bike and smacks a boy
And carries on spinning.
I said, 'Rev rev down the street,
I'll get you one more time!'
So the boy had enough and makes his own back
Plan well, bullying Jim could not jump any ramps.
The boy who was bullied he knows that's his weakness.
So next day all I could hear was
'Rev, rev down the street!
Coming to smack the boy
But jumps over the biggest ramp! He got scared -
And never started again.'
So that's the story of bullying Jim
(now vote for meeeeeeeeee!).

Tafari Bennett (11)
Cantrell Primary School

MERLIN'S MAGICAL LIFE

Merlin, Merlin,
He keeps whirlin'
He's having a shave
By his friend Clave.

Now he's got no beard
So he looks weird.
Merlin, Merlin,
He's stopped whirlin'.

Daniel Sweet (10)
Cantrell Primary School

DINNER DISASTER!

Yum! Yum!
Food for our tum,
Oh no, sausage roll,
Made with the cook's hairy mole.

Err! Gross!
A veggie nugget,
Quick, quick, let's bin it.

Get it off my plate,
Wriggly worms swimming in sauce
Disguised as spaghetti.
Guess who ate it?
Big belly Betty . . .

Err! Yuck!
Chocolate pud,
Made with the mushiest field mud!

What to drink today?
Get it away,
Lumpy milkshake
Made with seaweed from the lake!

Kathryn Dennis (11)
Cantrell Primary School

ICY WEATHER

Wrapping up warm days
Icy fingertips
Dripping icicle days
      Icy weather.

Cold snowman days
Slipping cars days
Skating on the ice days
      Icy weather.

Snowball days
Watering eyes days
Put the fire on days
      Icy weather.

No sun days
Hard grass days
Scraping noises days
      Icy weather.

Isabel Marriott (8)
Chetwynd Road Primary School

IMAGINE

Imagine a cat as small as a bat
Imagine an ox as small as a box
Imagine a flea as big as a bee
Imagine a dog as small as a frog
Imagine a pig wearing a wig
Imagine a pot as small as a dot
Imagine a rabbit with a bad habit.

William Stevenson (8)
Chetwynd Road Primary School

ICY WEATHER

Hot cocoa days
Snowball fight days
Car slipping days
  Icy weather.

Jumping on Mum's bed days
Playing on the PlayStation Days
Cold space days
  Icy weather.

Walking in the snowy flood days
Eye watering days
Cold penguin days
  Icy weather.

Scraping the window days
Chilly body days
Frozen bird days
  Icy weather.

Nippy nose days
Purple finger days
Icicle nose days
  Icy weather.

Leah Stone (8)
Chetwynd Road Primary School

ICY WEATHER

Frosty grass days
Rusty car days
Thick woolly coat days
      Icy weather.

Paths covered in ice days
Thick woolly sock days
White hot fire days
      Icy weather.

Eye watering days
Cars stuck in ice days
Snug mitten days
      Icy weather.

Doors bang open days
Windows frosted up days
Kettle boiling days
      Icy weather.

Emma Marshall (8)
Chetwynd Road Primary School

IMAGINE

Imagine an ox as smelly as socks
Imagine a bat as fat as a cat
Imagine a whale as small as a snail
Imagine a mouse as big as a house
Imagine a dog as tall as a log
Imagine a hare as long as a bear
Imagine a drake like a cake
Imagine but it will never happen.

Kieran Halpin (8)
Chetwynd Road Primary School

ICY WEATHER

Want it to be sunny days
Wrap up nice and warm days
Cold, glinting icicle days
      Icy weather.

Frozen up car days
People off school days
No more sun days
      Icy weather.

Gritter out last night days
Hard, crunchy grass days
Leaves falling off tree days
      Icy weather.

Frostbite finger days
Snuggling down in bed days
Fire on full blast days
      Icy weather.

No more sunny days
Slippy black ice days
No more PE days
      Icy weather.

Alexandra Springhall (8)
Chetwynd Road Primary School

ICY WEATHER

Scalding fire days
Skidding feet days
Icicles on your nose days
        Icy weather.

Ice skating days
Jumping in Mummy's bed days
Grit lying on the road days
        Icy weather.

Blazing fire days
Heather on fire days
Lips as blue as a bluebottle days
        Icy weather.

Joel Patchitt (7)
Chetwynd Road Primary School

ICY WEATHER

Get out of bed days
Grit on the road days
Blazing hot fire days
        Icy weather.

Under the duvet days
Slippy, slidy path days
Biting cold wind days
        Icy weather.

No outside PE days
Icicles everywhere days
People skidding everywhere days
        Icy weather.

Ben Wormald (7)
Chetwynd Road Primary School

ICY WEATHER

Fire red-hot days
Scraping car window days
Ice skating days
        Icy weather.

Snow like black ice days
Blizzard days
Snowflakes falling from sky days,
        Icy weather.

Building snowmen days
Snow like strawberry slush days
Frozen stiff car days
        Icy weather.

Jack Frost days,
Staying in bed days,
Gliding on icy days
        Icy weather.

Be careful days
Two quilt days
Going on sledge days
        Icy weather.

Wrapping up days
Raw days
Eyes water days
        Icy weather.

Snowdrift days
Snowball fight days
Looking for foxes days
        Icy weather.

Laurence Williamson (7)
Chetwynd Road Primary School

ICY WEATHER

Boiling cocoa days
Snowball fight days
Get wrapped in blanket days
                    Icy weather.

Biting the cold wind days
Crispy snowflake days
Stinging, tickling nose days
                    Icy weather.

Icy slippery ice days
Dusted with snow days
Bitter cold days
                    Icy weather.

Jack Frost days
Black ice days
Cold blizzard days
                    Icy weather.

Pouring down with hail days
Dazzling deep snow days
Slushy melted snow days
                    Icy weather.

Chelsea Grace (7)
Chetwynd Road Primary School

ICY WEATHER

Freezing windy days
Boiling hot food days
Ice skating cold days
        Icy weather

Wrap up warm days
Lay in bed days
Gritting road days
        Icy weather.

Slow walking days
Put on your hat days
Eyes watering days
        Icy weather.

Icy window days
Icy leaf days,
Get your coat days.
        Icy weathers.

Matthew Peall (7)
Chetwynd Road Primary School

ICY WEATHER

Nippy cold wind days
Cold snowman days
Frozen window days
        Icy weather.

Frozen road days
Turning icicles days
Scalding fires to warm
        Icy weather.

Tony Grimes (7)
Chetwynd Road Primary School

ICY WEATHER

Bitterly icy cold winter's days
Boiling hot fire days
Crunching icy cold grass days
       Icy weather.

Scraping icy cars days
Slippery cold icy days
Whirling cold icicle days
       Icy weather.

Icy leaves days
Slow walking days
Ice scattering days
       Icy weather.

Cold eyes watering days
Cold runny nose days
People tucked up warm in bed days
       Icy weather.

Icy cold windows days
Sliding feet days
Hot cocoa days
       Icy weather.

Emily Dainty (8)
Chetwynd Road Primary School

ICY WEATHER

Too icy for planes to land days
Crunchy grass days
Making snowmen days
      Icy weather.

Cars not starting up days
Winds being like hurricane days
Making footprint days
      Icy weather.

Blazing coal fire days
Staying in bed days
No school days
      Icy weather.

Ashley Hall (8)
Chetwynd Road Primary School

ICY WEATHER

Snuggling up in bed days
Playing out in BMX days
Icy icicles hanging from roofs days
      Icy weather.

Blizzard icy days
Snowflakes whirling round the play days
Stomping in the snow days
      Icy weather.

Black icy hailstone
Crashing down from the sky days
      Icy weather.

Emily Lupino-Poole (7)
Chetwynd Road Primary School

ICY WEATHER

Red nose days
Steamed up car days
Have a hot bath days
      Icy weather.

Crunching grass days
Gloves and scarves days
Frosty road days
      Icy weather.

Having a nice hot cup of cocoa days
Face turns purple or blue days
Frosty window days
      Icy weather.

Cold winter days
Sky turns grey days
Gets cold days.
      Icy weather.

Runny nose days
Frozen toe days
Frozen finger days
      Icy weather.

Katie Morrice (7)
Chetwynd Road Primary School

ICY WEATHER

Frosty ice days
Go in my bed days
      Icy weather.

Big claw ice days
Frozen ice cubes days
      Icy weather.

Crackling fire days
Icy bed days
Dribbly nose days
      Icy weather.

Raw fish days
Crunchy crab days
      Icy weather.

Cold ice skating days
Skating days
Ran on way days
      Icy weather.

Prickly cold days
Munchy ice days
      Icy weather.

Harvey Perttola *(7)*
Chetwynd Road Primary School

ICY WEATHER

Runny nose days
'Come on, get up' days
'Wrap up your scarf' days
        Icy weather.

Freezing crispy days
Raw sharp wind days
Icicles hanging off your nose days
        Icy weather.

White-hot blazing fire days
Icy blue finger days
Cup of warm cocoa days
        Icy weather.

Callum Henderson (8)
Chetwynd Road Primary School

ICY WEATHER

Four quilts days
Ice skating days
Jump in Mum's bed days
        Icy weather.

Go to the fire days
Extremely cold days
Sliding ice days
        Icy weather.

Icy cold days
Skidding ice days
Going ice boarding days
        Icy weather.

Kyle Thompson (8)
Chetwynd Road Primary School

ICY WEATHER

Trying to make snowmen days
Looking for foxes days
Making angels days
      Icy weather

Rolling in icy places days
Sledge playing days
Sliding on ice days
      Icy weather.

Having snowball fights days
Making footprints days
Car stiff days
      Icy weather.

Having Ready Brek days
Having hot dinner days
Car not starting days.
      Icy weather.

Sam Mansfield (7)
Chetwynd Road Primary School

IMAGINE

Imagine a flea as big as a bee
Imagine a rat as fat as a cat
Imagine a dog jump as high as a frog
      Imagine

Imagine a flea as big as a bee
Imagine a bear as small as a hare
Imagine a dodo as intelligent as a doe
Imagine an ox as weak as a box.
      Imagine.

Christopher Waddington (9)
Chetwynd Road Primary School

ICY WEATHER

White noses turning red days
Don't forget your hat days
Sitting by the baking hot fire days
      Icy weather.

Shaking icy finger days
Watering eyes days
Practising ice skating days
      Icy weather.

Staying in bed days
Indoor play days
Watch out for black ice days
      Icy weather.

Snow turning into ice days
Sharp icicles hanging over the roof days
Grit on the road days
      Icy weather.

Sitting watching TV days
Breaking ankles days
Putting two quilts on the bed days
      Icy weather.

Animals in their cosy cages days
People staying in bed days
No more late bedtime days
      Icy weather.

Hot chocolate days
Snowball fight days
Frosted over car days
      Icy weather.

Nose running days
Not very well days
Wishing I was on holiday days

Icy weather!

Sarah Buckley (8)
Chetwynd Road Primary School

ICY WEATHER

Raw wind days
Kettle boiling days
Sea turns to ice days
    Icy weather.

Paths covered in ice days
Children watching, entertaining TV days
Delicious warm good food days
    Icy weather.

Staying in bed days
Frosty, chilly, nippy days
Rusty, old car breakdown days
    Icy weather.

Sweet children stay in days
Snug mitten days
Doors iced-up days
    Icy weather.

Windows bang open days
Crunching snow days
White-hot fire days
    Icy weather.

Charlotte Pick (7)
Chetwynd Road Primary School

IMAGINE

Imagine a frog, as big as a dog
Imagine a warthog, the weight of a log
Imagine an ox, as small as a box
Imagine a hare, as loud as a bear

> Imagine
> Imagine
> Imagine

Imagine a snail, as large as a whale
Imagine a cat, the size of a hat
Imagine an iguana, as green as an unripe banana
Imagine a goat, as wet as a boat.

> Imagine
Imagine a mouse, as tall as a house
> Imagine
> Imagine

> Imagine that.

Ahranee Canden (8)
Chetwynd Road Primary School

IMAGINE

Imagine some mice, as thin as woodlice
Imagine a whale, as small as a snail
Imagine a house, as white as a mouse
Imagine a goat, as wet as a boat
Imagine a hare, as strong as a bear
Imagine an iguana, as green as a not ripe banana
And finally . . .
Imagine a rhyme, as funny as mine.

Thomas Corcoran (8)
Chetwynd Road Primary School

IMAGINE

Imagine a fox, as smelly as socks
Imagine a frog, as fat as a log
Imagine a ram, as small as a lamb
Imagine an ox, square like a box.
      Imagine that
      Imagine that.

Imagine a cat, as blind as a bat
Imagine a gnat, as flat as a mat
Imagine a drake, as round as a cake
Imagine a mouse, as big as a house.
      What else will come up?
      What else will come up?
      I don't know
      I don't know.

Nila Rochester (9)
Chetwynd Road Primary School

IMAGINE THIS

Imagine a dodo, as unique as a dino
Imagine a sword, as sharp as a croc's tooth
Imagine a goat, as wet as a boat
Imagine a whale, as small as a snail.
      Imagine

Imagine a mouse, as big as a house
Imagine a fish, as dry as a dish
Imagine a bat, as huge as a cat
Imagine a cheetah as warm as a heater
And finally . . .
Imagine a rhyme as dippy as mine.

Christopher Gray (9)
Chetwynd Road Primary School

IMAGINE

Imagine a rat as fat as a cat
Imagine a snail as big as a whale
Imagine a boar as small as an apple core
Imagine a dog as bouncy as a frog.

   Imagine

Imagine a fox as smelly as socks
Imagine a fish as round as a dish
Imagine a flea, as big as a bee
Imagine an eagle as silly as a seagull.

   Imagine.

Imagine a dog as hairy as a warthog
Imagine a goat as wet as a boat
Imagine a mouse as tall as a house
Imagine a hare as huge as a bear.

Charlotte Hughes (9)
Chetwynd Road Primary School

IMAGINE

Imagine a snail as fat as a whale
Imagine a fox as smelly as socks
Imagine a fish as large as a dish
Imagine a boar as brown as a core
Imagine a seal as small as an eel
Imagine a hare as big as a bear
Imagine a goat as wet as a boat
Imagine a log as thin as a dog
Imagine a bat as fat as a rat.

   But it won't be that.

Samuel Hands (8)
Chetwynd Road Primary School

IMAGINE

Imagine an ant as big as an Indian tea plant
Imagine a boar as small as an apple core
Imagine a cat as flat as a mat
Imagine a drake as yummy as a cake
      Imagine that!
      Just imagine.

Imagine an eagle as silly as a seagull
Imagine a fish as round as a dish
Imagine a goat, as calm as a musical note
Imagine a hare, as grumpy as a grizzly bear
      Imagine a rhyme
      As fine as mine.

Elizabeth Jones (9)
Chetwynd Road Primary School

IMAGINE

Imagine a fox putting on smelly socks
Imagine a rabbit wearing a habit
Imagine a goose as brown as a moose
Imagine a whale playing with a snail

      Imagine

Imagine a fish eating out from a dish
Imagine a bear as hairy as a hare
Imagine an ox as tall as a fox
Imagine a snake as wide as a lake.

      Imagine.

Lydia Youle (8)
Chetwynd Road Primary School

IMAGINE

Imagine a bat, as big as a cat
Imagine a hare, as rough as a bear
Imagine a dog, as fat as a warthog
Imagine a snail, as sharp as hail.

      Imagine.

Imagine a bee, as small as a flea
Imagine a worm, as mean as a germ
Imagine a mouse, as tall as a house
Imagine a cat, as flat as a mat.

      Imagine

Imagine a goose that eats chocolate moose
Imagine a fox, as smelly as socks
Imagine a fish, as dry as a dish
Imagine a poem, as funny as this.

Sophie Naylor (8)
Chetwynd Road Primary School

IMAGINE

Imagine an ox as big as a bin box
Imagine a goat as light as a stoat
Imagine a dog which can jump like a frog
Imagine a cat as big as a bat
        Imagine.

Imagine a dog as fat as a warthog
Imagine a hare as fat as a bear
Imagine a foal as soft as a mole
Imagine a fox as strong as an ox
        Imagine that.

Ross Osborne (9)
Chetwynd Road Primary School

IMAGINE

Imagine a cat as big as a bat
Imagine a boar as brown as an apple core
Imagine a gnat as flat as a mat
Imagine a dog as bouncy as a frog.
      Imagine

Imagine a flea as huge as a bee
Imagine a goat as wet as a boat
Imagine a hare as big as a bear
Imagine a mouse as big as a house.
      Imagine

Imagine an iguana as large as a piranha
Imagine a rat as warm as a hat
Imagine a snail as big as a whale
Imagine a dog as hairy as a warthog.
      Imagine.

Charlotte Brick (9)
Chetwynd Road Primary School

IMAGINE

Imagine a gnat as fat as a cat
Imagine a bee as small as a flea
Imagine a dog as bouncy as a frog
Imagine a mole as fast as a foal.
      Imagine

Imagine a mouse as tall as a house
Imagine a snail as blue as a whale
Imagine a goat as light as a float
Imagine a rat as black as a bat.
      Imagine.

Zoe Cook (8)
Chetwynd Road Primary School

IMAGINE

Imagine a stoat, as heavy as a goat
Imagine an ox, as sly as a fox
Imagine a yeti, as boring as a jetty
Imagine a foal, as smooth as a mole
  Imagine
  Imagine

Imagine an eagle, as fluffy as a beagle
Imagine a drake, as yummy as a cake
Imagine a gnat, as slick as a cat,
  Imagine
  Imagine
  Imagine

Imagine a moose, as small as a goose
Imagine an iguana, as nippy as a banana
  Imagine
  Imagine
  Imagine
  Imagine

Imagine an eel as fat as a seal
  Imagine!

Josh Knight (9)
Chetwynd Road Primary School

WHO AM I?

A sky sailor
A feather mailer

An egg layer
A home stayer

A nut cracker
A tree smacker

A bread eater
A worm beater

A morning waker
A nest maker

A superb lander
A small feather panda

A feather ball
Who'll never fall

All of this stirred
And you get a

Bird.

Stephanie Blanco (10)
Cloudside Junior School

SPACE

S pace is a never-ending place with lots of
P lanets inside, but none in our
A tmosphere and the moon
C ircles the
E arth.

Joseph Oldham (11)
Cloudside Junior School

THIS PERSON IS . . .

This person is a crusty piece of paper
He is a spicy curry with red-hot chilli peppers
He is out of date milk with fungi
He is a bad tempered thunderstorm
He is a deep black panther
He is a skeleton getting up from his grave
He is a grumpy 3.00 in the morning
He is an insensitive ghost
He is a bloodthirsty murder
He is an unlikely angel with a curse
He is an action-packed horror film.

This person is a comfortable sofa
She is a feather floating from a fluffy cloud
She is an angel of goodness
She is a hardworking wrestler
She is a sweet coconut drink
She is a curry with lots of rice
She is a panda with a fluffy coat
She is a yellow with a splash of pink
She is an action-packed romantic film.

Jared Pointer (11)
Cloudside Junior School

WHAT IS A PIANO?

A piano is a set of dirty teeth,
It's sometimes thunder in a rainstorm,
Or birds chirping on a summer's day.
A piano is a lot of black and white
building blocks in a row,
It is the coat of a zebra, alone on a field.

Neomi Ryan (10)
Cloudside Junior School

HISTORY HORROR!

Elizabeth is all for peace
but her sister Mary wants this to cease
Henry is a great ruler but with his
clothes he could be cooler.

Anne Boleyn had an extra finger
but she wasn't a very good singer.
Edward her brother is just another.
King Henry VIII has not a lover
because he chopped off Anne Boleyn's head
and now she's dead.

A short name can be 'Tudy'
The Tudors can be sort of moody.
So Henry has to get with the trend
but now I'm afraid my poem has to end.

Ashley Mather (9)
Cloudside Junior School

SPACE

Rockets shooting into space
Flying through the sky
It leaves the base
And begins to fly
Rockets in space.

There are thousands of stars
And one of the planets is Mars
They look dead small
But they're very tall
Stars in the sky.

James Brooks (10)
Cloudside Junior School

EMILY

Who hurt people and was abducted by aliens.

Beep, beep goes the alarm on Emily's car
She's off to the really cool bar
Promised her dad she'd dance with him
But then she met this boy called Tim.

Goodnight Dad, goodnight bar
As she gets into his car
He drives down the street
And guess who she meets?

But Dameon a first class star
She falls put of the car and onto the tar
Tim looks at the floor and turns all green and scaly
She looks up and sees her cousin Hayley.

The alien sees her knobbly knees and turns away in anger
He turns round without a sound and slowly, slowly kills her.

Kirsten Langley (9)
Cloudside Junior School

THIS PERSON IS A ...

This person is a comfy sofa
He is a dark blue
He is a dark black puma
He is a big interactive robot
He is a 12am sharpy person
He is a fizzy pint of Guinness
He is a greasy steak and chips
He is a storm
He is a horror film.

Jamie Beasley (11)
Cloudside Junior School

THE ALIENS

The aliens in their mothership
plan to invade Planet Earth
'We will attack tomorrow at
11 o'clock in the morning.'

The aliens had yellow bodies, green eyes
cone-shaped heads, orange beards and really
goofy teeth. 'Let's go then lads, we will
soon have power over the blunt heads.'

So they attacked at 11 o'clock
but they did not last long.
After they landed in a field
surrounded by scary, straw, wooden men.

'Blast it, we lost again, we are not as brave as we thought.
Oh well, there's always next year.'

Ryan Yaxley (10)
Cloudside Junior School

THIS PERSON IS . . .

A comfy chair
The colour grey
A cheetah ready to pounce
A bolt of lightning
4.00 - time to go mad
A pint of Budweiser
A hot dog
An eclipse
The Mummy.

Scott Riley (10)
Cloudside Junior School

THE MAN WHO HIT HIS HEAD

The man who hit his head
Climbing out his bed.
He walks down the stairs
And has a scrap with some bears.
He jumps out the door
And falls on a wild boar.
The boar takes him to the shop
And he has to do the hop.
He went in the shop for his leg
But instead bought a nice long peg.
He walks down to the chippy
And finds a dead cool hippy.
He gets on the hippy's bike
And goes to a shop called Strike.
The man doesn't know how to get home from Strike
But the hippy has gone on his bike . . .

Ashley Stocks (9)
Cloudside Junior School

THIS PERSON IS . . .

Is a fluffy king-sized bed
She is a light purple
She is an incredibly intelligent dolphin
She is a full notepad
She is 6.55 in the morning
She is a smouldering cup of coffee
She is a spicy chicken and mushroom curry
She is the boiling sun in the Sahara
She is the film 'Titanic'.

Benjamin Brandon (10)
Cloudside Junior School

WHY ME?

'Come here,' says my mum
'Help me get the washing in.'
'Huh . . . why me?' I say.

'Help!' shouts Dad roaring
'Come and wash the car,' he says
'Huh . . . why me?' I say.

'Read me a story!
Read me this,' says my brother.
'Huh . . . why me?' I say.

'Come here dear,' says Gran
'Help me cook your roast dinner,'
'Huh . . . why me?' I say.

'It's not fair,' I say.
'I have to do all the work.
Huh . . . why me?' I say.

Emma Billinger (9)
Cloudside Junior School

THIS PERSON IS . . .

This person is a cuddly fluffy sofa
He is bright blue
He is a fluffy dog, ready to run
He is a weight trainer
He is bright and early 6am.
He is a water fountain
He is a burning steak like the sun
He is a bright blue sky
He is a kick-boxing film.

Jessica Garton (10)
Cloudside Junior School

SCHOOL'S GONE

Children scream, teachers leap
Schools gone, yippee
Go home, call on the phone
To all of my friends
The day nearly ends.

'Going out Mum, see ya Dad.'
'Where are you going at this time of night?'
'I'm going out to start a fight.'
Dad goes mad, calls me bad
Mum says, 'Have a good time.'

Finally the week has ended
Splendid!
I can't wait to get back to school
Being off has started to get uncool.

Off I go, shut the door
Now the poem is no more.

Hannah Holton (10)
Cloudside Junior School

THIS PERSON IS . . .

This person is a tall lamp, with a pink fluffy lampshade
She is a pink with a touch of lilac
She is a tall long giraffe which touches the sky
She is a vacuum cleaner that's never off
She is a 12.30 in the afternoon
She is a glass of cherryade all fizzy and nice
She is a vanilla ice cream with a cherry on top
She is a rainbow beautiful and bright
She is a miniature Buffy!

Samantha Weatherley (11)
Cloudside Junior School

TIGER TIGER

It prowls closer and closer,
I can hear it breathing louder and louder
It's got razor-sharp teeth
And eyes like green lasers.
Big tall trees stand proudly
The ground is covered with leaves.

It's getting closer, I can hear its feet
Plodding along the floor getting hungrier by the minute.
I wonder what it wants for tea?
Maybe it wants me!

I'm running as fast as thunder,
It's chasing me.
Its claws like needles
I can imagine them digging into me.
It turns and walks away
I am so relieved
But all of a sudden
It's in front of me waiting to
Gobble me down!

Melissa McEvoy (9)
Cloudside Junior School

THIS PERSON IS . . .

This person is a furry sofa
She is a bright yellow with a touch of orange
She is a hamster on a wheel
She is a bouncing ball flying at a pace
She is 8.30am ready for school
She is a fizzy Coca-Cola ready to whizz
She is a Monday morning bright sun.

Hayley Brown (11)
Cloudside Junior School

LADY MACBETH

L ovely and wicked
A nd very persuasive
D evious very
Y ou wouldn't want her as your wife.

M acbeth deserved better
A nd she plotted to kill
C urious and sneaky
B eautiful but different inside
E ven though she was beautiful she's got a temper
T empted and did what she wanted
H orrible to everyone except Macbeth.

Eleanor Moss (10)
Cloudside Junior School

THIS PERSON IS . . .

A teacher's pet
She is curly and brown
She is a ginger kitten
She is a purple footstool with pink spots
She is 3.30pm at the end of school
She is fish, chips and mushy peas
She is rain with a streak of thunder
She is a funny action-packed film
She is a bubbly cocktail
Shaken not stirred.

Rhiannon Holdway (10)
Cloudside Junior School

HIP HOP HAP IT'S THE YEAR 3 RAP

Rap about a flying ball
Rap about when you fall
Rap about the trees so tall
Rap about the smelly hall.

Rap about me and you
Rap about the cows that moo
Rap about a football pitch
Rap about the dirty ditch.

Rap about my brilliant house
Rap about the running mouse
Rap about the Mini car
Rap about the shining star.

Jack Appleyard & Liam Osbiston (7)
Cloudside Junior School

THIS PERSON IS . . .

An oak wardrobe full of clothes
She is a West Highland terrier
She is a deep red
She is an expensive pair of Italian shoes
She is an early morning
She is a Baileys on the rocks
She is a toasted piglet
She is a sunny day in Australia
She is a romantic comedy with a happy ending.

Sophie Douglas (10)
Cloudside Junior School

THE SEA

I sit on the shore
and listen to the gentle waves overtake each other.

I look at the deep red sky
and see the sun start to set

As I feel the golden sand on my body
I watch the fish swim freely

With my bucket, I pick up the rocky coral and the beautiful shells
and hold them preciously

Then I go for a snorkel
and go below all of the seaweed

Then I go back to my home
Oh that was a lovely day!

Liam Seals (11)
Cloudside Junior School

THIS PERSON IS . . .

This person is . . .

A tall, stretched up, black lamp
The colour blue with a twist of yellow
A long-necked giraffe stretching up to the top of the trees
A smooth table
She is 7.30 in the morning
A big glass of Coke
A hot spicy curry ready to eat
She is the sun sizzling on a hot day
A spinning disco dancer.

Lauren Sheppard (10)
Cloudside Junior School

THE HAWK AND THE SHREW

In the rocky mountains with the green moss
The shrews are running around
Taking no caution to the stalker watching
They did not know it, but a hawk was watching them.
For the hawk waited, glided and grabbed one, and ate it for its tea.
But then one shrew spotted the hawk staring down on them.
It raised the alarm, but one shrew would not budge.
The shrew was a sitting duck.
The hawk saw the shrew, it went to it like a moth to a flame.
It swooped down on the shrew and got its claws ready.
The hawk took the shrew out in one shot
Ripping it up in pieces.
It took it back to its nest, it was a river of blood.
That night the hawk had a feast.
If the shrew would have watched a bit more, it would not have
happened.
Let this be a lesson to you in life; be more careful and pay more
attention because someone is always watching.

Harry Daykin (9)
Cloudside Junior School

THIS PERSON IS . . .

This person is a squishy sofa
She is a colourful pink and purple fan
She is a dolphin soft and smooth
She is a pencil in a pencil case
She is a Monday at 8am
She is a bottle of strawberry squash
She is a chicken tikka kebab
She is the sun in the sky
She is a big book of poems.

Portia Richmond (11)
Cloudside Junior School

HIP HOP HAP IT'S THE YEAR 3 RAP

Rap about something small
Rap about something tall
Rap about something free
Rap about the number three.

Rap about the barking dogs
Rap about the prickly logs
Rap about the playground wall
Rap about the dinner hall.

Rap about the broken fence
Rap about the dirty pence
Rap about the swimming pool
Rap about something cool.

Rap about the yellow door
Rap about the smelly floor
Rap about a bossy king
Rap about a diamond ring.

Gemma Bestwick & Zoe Lee (8)
Cloudside Junior School

THIS PERSON IS ...

This person is a comfy leather piece of furniture
She is the reddest rose
She is the cutest tiger
She is a furry cushion,
She is 12 o'clock ready to pounce
She is the fizz in pop
She is a lovely spaghetti Bolognese
She is a red sunset
She is a romantic film.

Adam Westwick (10)
Cloudside Junior School

YEAH, IT'S PLAY TIME

Yeah it's play time
We're full of joy
We go out and play
With our favourite toy.

We're running about
As we please
Then we fall over
And graze our knees.

Oh no, the bell has rung,
Is this the end of our fun?
As we go in we start to cry,
To the playground
We say bye-bye.

Sophie Dunstan (10)
Cloudside Junior School

THIS PERSON IS . . .

This person is an arm of a chair with no cover
He is jet-black
He is a cheetah racing for the kill
He is an overpowered motorbike
He is a 2 o'clock ready for football
He is flat pineapple juice
He is a slice of thin pizza covered with pepperoni
He is a sunny afternoon
He is a never-ending action movie!

Thomas Warren (10)
Cloudside Junior School

BRACES

At first I thought a
Brace would be great
But when I got out of
The dentist, I looked quite a state.

My mouth hung open in all that pain
Working out how to talk
As I walked down the lane.

I have to leave it out
For swimming and PE
And people who don't have braces
Shriek at the metal monster, believe me!

Having a brace is quite inconvenient
And I am very, truly relieved
That it's not permanent.

Rebecca Pearce (10)
Cloudside Junior School

THIS PERSON IS . . .

A messed up desk
He is a light blue
He is a robin
He is a big rock
He is 12.00 midday
He is an extra large can of beer
He is a Big Mac
He is a sunny day
He is Scooby-Doo.

Jacob Ridge (11)
Cloudside Junior School

OFSTED

OFSTED are cruel
And very uncool
They're really mean
And just too clean
They eat carrots
And talk more than parrots
They inspect our schools
And think we're fools
They're really bad
And make me mad
OFSTED are really cruel.

Thomas Appleyard (10)
Cloudside Junior School

THIS PERSON IS . . .

He is a hard stained floor
He is a dark deep red
He is an angry mad tiger
He is a muscular action man
He is a 12am active man
He is a bubbly pint of lager
He is a stringy spaghetti Bolognese
He is a bright sunny day
He is an action-packed army film.

Matthew Roberts (11)
Cloudside Junior School

THE SKY

The sky is a dark chocolate bar
ready to be swallowed.

It's pitch-black paper
with diamonds scattered over it.

At daytime the clouds are cosy cushions
of fluffy candyfloss!

At night the moon is sat in the sky,
has someone actually kicked a ball of cheese up there?

As the night-time darkness eats the daylight
the world goes silent!

Gemma Standring (11)
Cloudside Junior School

THIS PERSON IS . . .

This person is a soft teddy bear sofa
She is bright yellow like the sun
She is a cuddly teddy bear
She is a sparkling gold pencil case
She is half-past twelve midday
She is a gleaming glass of lemon and lime juice
She is a McDonald's Happy Meal
She is the refreshing sun
She is the Teletubbies.

Hannah Woods (10)
Cloudside Junior School

ME AND MY SISTER

Me and my sister always fight
You're more likely to find us fighting at night
We punch and kick
Make each other sick
We also never get along.

She's always acting like a pain
Right now she's making me go insane
Sometimes she can be mad
All the time she can be bad
We also never get along.

Mum and Dad always shout at her
Then look at me and give a purr
I think after all she's not that bad
And does look a tad sad
Although we fight
She's quite alright.

Kelly Bestwick (10)
Cloudside Junior School

THIS PERSON IS . . .

She is a groovy chick lampshade
She is a bright purple tin of paint
She is a dolphin diving through a hoop
She is a sparkly flower pencil case
She is 12.30 dinner time
She is a lemon, lime and mango cocktail
She is a large portion of chips
She is a sunny Portugal sun
She is a Jacqueline Wilson bad girls book
She is Lara Croft from Tomb Raider.

Natalie Wearing (10)
Cloudside Junior School

OFSTED INSPECTORS

The inspectors were scary
All horrible and mean
Their faces were wrinkly
And their feet were green.

We were all shivering
Sat in our chairs
We were working hard
As they gave us funny glares.

They look like demons
With big jelly eyes
Their noses stick out
And their heads are like pies.

When they left
The only thing we could say
Was bye-bye inspectors
Hip, hip, hooray!

Chris Wakefield (11)
Cloudside Junior School

THIS PERSON IS . . .

This person is a big cuddly sofa
She is a light sweet red
She is a soft panda
She is a tidy bed
She is 7.30 bright and early
She is a hot cup of tea in the morning
She is a healthy salad
She is a rainbow in the sparkling sky
She is a romantic film.

Melissa Jones (11)
Cloudside Junior School

HIP HOP HAP IT'S THE YEAR 3 RAP

Rap about my messy room
Rap about sweeping with a broom
Rap about the front wall
Rap about our school hall.

Rap about red ketchup
Rap about a little cup
Rap about the birds that sing
Rap about a wedding ring.

Rap about a kiss on the lips
Rap about forward flips
Rap about a broken fence
Rap about my lost two pence.

Georgina Grainger (7) & Kayleigh Davis (8)
Cloudside Junior School

THIS PERSON IS . . .

This person is a soft fluffy bouncy chair
She is the colour of the sparkling sun
She is a soft cuddly puppy
She is a warm blanket to you away from the cold
She is a bright early morning
She is cups of Coke with ice in it
She is a vegetarian meal
She is a sparkling blue sea
She is a funny film.

Jade Nicholson (10)
Cloudside Junior School

HIP HOP HAP IT'S THE YEAR 3 RAP

Rap about the smelly hall
Rap about the cage so tall
Rap about the marching kids
Rap about the dustbin lids.

Rap about the rotten egg
Rap about my sister Meg
Rap about my lucky charms
Rap about the dirty farms.

Rap about your spotty face
Rap about up in space
Rap about the witch's nose
Rap about Mary's toes.

Abigail O'Loughlin (7) & Charlotte Harris (8)
Cloudside Junior School

CHRISTMAS

It is Christmas Eve
I get Santa a mince pie
and a drink of Coke.

I go up the stairs
and get into my bunk bed
and fall straight to sleep.

I wake up early
and gallop down the staircase
'Presents!' I shout.

Honor Duff (10)
Cloudside Junior School

THE PHOENIX!

Feathers like gold, shining in the sun,
Raging fire from its beak crying out madness
Its eyes shouting horror to all he could see
Feet like claws ripping its food apart to pieces!

Swooping off the cliff to find nearby sticks for nesting
People gazing around like they've seen a ghost
Kids in streets run to their mums saying they've seen a gold-
Pterodactyl
Most just stare in wonder!

It's laid eggs, come to home, come to safety,
Warmed and looked after by their mum,
Until the day comes they will be baby phoenixes
But still that won't be till a long time!

Splish splash splish splash goes the wet bath in the nearest river,
The phoenix tries to catch fish swimming past him
Coming up to night-time *whoosh* back up to her home
Cosy, warmed, up to her home snuggled up to her den!

Oh no it's winter, oh no it's time for hibernation,
Although the phoenix is a fine bird, it still can warm the little ones,
Oh no it's raining, oh no it's thundering, the phoenix will lose its fire
Phew it's stopped finally!

Springtime is here at last, look the phoenixes are hatched,
Now mother phoenix has got to get some food for them
To live and grow up like real phoenixes!

Kariss Miles (10)
Cloudside Junior School

THE DAY IT RAINED CATS AND DOGS

One day I went outside and what did I find?
It was raining cats and dogs,
It was raining cats and dogs,
I went outside and what did I find?
It was raining cats and dogs.

It was coming down like stones
Coming down like stones,
Coming down like stones
And one hit me on the head.

Then I went back inside and I wished it wasn't happening,
not happening,
not happening,
I wished it wasn't happening, and then something happened.

Then I woke up in bed,
in bed,
in bed,
I woke up in bed and it was only a dream.

Clare Billington (9)
Cloudside Junior School

ROLLER COASTER RIDE

I'm on the roller coaster, tumbling and turning
Watching all the trees go by just like years.
I feel as cold as ice and as warm as the sun,
Laughing and laughing having so much fun!

I'm in a tunnel, it's dark and damp
Watching the light at the other side,
I feel soft and friendly whizzing by
'I want another go, another try!'

Louise Brace (9)
Cloudside Junior School

PARENTS

Parents, what are they like?
Always shouting
Ever so boring.
Oh no, here they come
Ahhh look at my mum.
She looks really mad
Have I been bad?
Will she shout?
What's it about?
She walked straight past me
What have I done?
She's heading for my brother
'Oh no, Isaac, run!'

Rose Heppell (10)
Cloudside Junior School

QUEEN

Children scream down my street
What's all the noise about?
Oh yes I remember where's my treat?
Yes the Queen's coming for tea.
We are having pizza and peas
The Queen's here,
Then she goes
Bye bye Queen
Come back soon.

Lucy Dinsdale (9)
Cloudside Junior School

THE GHOST TRAIN

I got on the ghost train
I was really, really scared.
But my mum was there beside me
And the train started and off we went.

We went through a tunnel
Which was as colourful as a rainbow
It made me feel really dizzy
And I'd just had a drink which was really fizzy.

Next we went through a spooky place
And a skeleton came behind me,
And he covered my face!
Then I heard a noise which sounded like a ghost!
            Oooooohhhh!

When we got out of there I waved to my dad
The train was slowing down which made me feel sad.
I thought that it was as scary as a haunted house
So I got out of the train and went to the next ride.

Holly Jennings (10)
Cloudside Junior School

HOLIDAY AT THE BEACH

The beach is a burning sun
A golden door to paradise
A soft marshmallow under your feet
The beach is a loaf of brown bread
With pebbles everywhere you tread
The beach is a food for the great big jaws of the sea
Look around, what a sight
I am definitely coming here again!

Stephen Allison (11)
Cloudside Junior School

TREES

Trees swaying from side to side
Leaves falling to the ground
Softly clattering on the floor
Down, down, down.

In the morning wind
Trees bend and go *snap*
Clatter, bang, crash,
On the muddy path.

Trees can be dangerous
If you're under them when they fall
They can easily kill people
Tiny, big or small.

Trees can be lots of different sizes
Tiny, big or small
With branches sticking out everywhere,
All crumbly, brown and bare.

Everywhere I look there's always a tree
Sometimes I think they're looking at me
They're such fascinating things
They help us to breathe,
That's one thing they can achieve.

They come in colours from green to red
To yellow to brown
All of them spread their roots
Underground.
I feel sorry for the little birds
When people chop down their trees
Because that's where they live
That's where they nest
That's where they breed.

Kimberley Squires (10)
Cloudside Junior School

FOOTBALL

My name is Johnathon Slack
I always like to hack
I love to play football
I always hear the parents call
'Get on the pitch and do your best'
Our team never gets a rest.
I wish I was rich
The problem about our pitch
Is that it is so lumpy.
If we lose the manager's always grumpy.
Our team is so rubbish
All the books I've got are never published.
I've never scored before
I've always been poor.
I am thick because I banged my head on the door.
I always wish I was a professional
Their goals are sensational
I always like to lie
At football I never try
That's the story about Johnathon Slack
Who always likes to hack.

Johnathon Slack (9)
Cloudside Junior School

FOOTBALL MATCH!

We kick off
Jordan slices the ball up field
Johnny runs on to it like a steam train.
The goalie comes out and snatches the ball
Like a prowling tiger.

We're on top of our game as we score.
'Hooray!' shouts the crowd.
Peep
Half-time.

Our manager is happy
'Keep it up,' he says
We go out for half number two
But disaster, they score
Noooooo!

We kick off again
We race up field
As Zach smacks it into the back of the net.
Seconds later
Peep, peep, peep
We've won! Yes!

Daniel Brookes (10)
Cloudside Junior School

MY DAD

My dad is a builder
He works all day
When he gets up in the morning
His hair is like rotten hay.

He draws the curtains
And then he goes down the stairs
He takes his bowl to the worktop
And fills it with rotten hairs!

Then he gets out the milk
And pours in the whole jug
He drinks the milky hairs
And he gets out his mug.

He puts his mug under the tap
And twists the hexagon-shaped knob.
Water pours in like waterfalls
But he quickly switches it off.

He runs up the stairs
And gets on his layers of clothes.
He runs out the house like a flash
And round to the building site he goes.

As he works all day
The sun gets lower,
Watching the horizon across the sky,
Dad travels home to do all the fun tomorrow.

Nicola Bilbie (10)
Cloudside Junior School

BEWARE THE BATTLE OF BOSWORTH

I walk onto the field, the grass tickles my feet
You have to stand, there's no seat.

They parade onto the field, stand still and straight
My, my, they do look great.

Charging, running at each other
Not like play fighting with your brother.

Arrows shooting in the sky
Some people are bound to die.

Blood laying on the floor
Rich and red just like a bright red door.

Richard charges over to death
There's no relief.

Stabbing him down, now he's dead
And the crown fell off his head.

Henry ruled for a long time
But now it's time to say 'Goodbye.'

Danielle Nelson (9)
Cloudside Junior School

AN EXPLODING CONVERSATION

'Jonny,' bellowed his mum angrily,
'Come up here, now!'
'Coming, Mum,' said Jonny happily unaware,
'What's the problem Mum?'
Then he saw the steam sprouting from her ears!
He froze on the spot
'This room looks like a bombsite!' exploded his mum.

Jessica Bavin (11)
Cloudside Junior School

FRIENDS

Friends are there for you when you're sad
They help you out when everything's bad
Sometimes you fall out
Sometimes you shout
But you always make up in the end.

Friends can be a bit daft
And they always make you laugh
Sometimes they're lazy
Sometimes they're crazy
And sometimes they drive you round the bend.

Gemma France (10)
Cloudside Junior School

TEENAGER

Boy lover
Movie lover
Geek hater
Groovy dancer
Poem lover
Teacher hater
Spotty facer
Blonde streaker
Make-up monster
That's my sister.

Gary Beach (10)
Cloudside Junior School

MY SISTER AND ME

People say it is very strange
That my sister and I act a different age
Get on together and never fall out
You'll never see us scream or shout.

If you come round for some tea
We will sit there happily
We are like two best friends
I hope this friendship never ends.

Now you know about my sister and me
But that's the end of my true story.

Sophie Edmonds (10)
Cloudside Junior School

BARRY

Night waker
Heart breaker
Rattle thrower
Bubble blower
Nasty trumper
Hard thumper
Loud crier
Little liar
Smiling toothless creature.

Adam Palmer (11)
Cloudside Junior School

MY IMAGINATION

My imagination is a
most exciting thing
I can be a cloud
or one that can sing!

I can have a world
that belongs to only me
My imagination is so wide
I can choose what to be!

I have a huge quantity
of ideas, things from books
I could be a vampire or ghost
and give very nasty looks!

I could be in a fun fairy tale
or be as slow and slimy
as a slippery snail!

But my imagination has to step quickly
because there's nothing
I like better than being me!

Laura Ames (11)
Cloudside Junior School

SCHOOL

S   ilence in the classroom, silence in the yard
C   arefully we walk in lines
H   oping that the teachers won't shout at us
O   pening the door to the classroom
O   h what fun we're going to have
L   esson time comes along and we all work harder than ever.

Gemma Ames (11)
Cloudside Junior School

WHAT A DAY

Yes, school's out
Let's shout, shout, shout.

I walk right up to the gate
To meet me old good mate.

I get into the car
'Why hello Grandma.'

I park in the front yard
My brother had a mard.

'What's up brother?'
'I want to see my mother.'

Oh no I tripped in some mud
And snapped me little football stud.

Outside I wait for my mum
The house, well, looks pretty glum.

Mum opens the door
And the story is no more.

Dameon Taylor (10)
Cloudside Junior School

HORSES

H   orses are fun
O   n the green grass
R   unning at top speed
S   winging their legs up and down
E   ating the lush green grass
S   taggering around.

Leanne Smith (10)
Cloudside Junior School

THE OCEAN IS . . .

The ocean is   a giant's bath
a great path.

a fish world
a tail curled.

a sand raker
a wave breaker.

a shell singer
a boat bringer.

Leigh Feranti (11)
Cloudside Junior School

TRUFFLE (MY HAMSTER)

My hamster is a little sweetie
A caramel dipped in milk chocolate
He is a teddy
Squidgy and soft
He is a star
A shining light
He is my ray of sunlight
That wakes me in the morning
He is my hamster, Truffle.

Victoria Block (11)
Cloudside Junior School

HIP HOP HAP IT'S THE YEAR 3 RAP

Rap about the waves at sea
Rap about the brilliant tea
Rap about the birds so high
Rap about the diamond sky.

Rap about the basketball
Rap about the dining hall
Rap about the swimming pool
Rap about the man so cool.

Rap about the shiny stars
Rap about the planet Mars
Rap about the fireman
Rap about the rolling can.

Rap about the brilliant school
Rap about the caretaker's tool
Rap about the people's walk
Rap about the children's talk.

Rap about the horse and cart
Rap about the gin that's smart
Rap about the speeding cars
Rap about shining bars.

Vikki Brooks & Chloe Featherstone (7)
Cloudside Junior School

HIP HOP HAP IT'S A YEAR 3 RAP

Rap about the school wall
Rap about playing ball
Rap about going outside
Rap about playing hide.

Rap about a rusty key
Rap about you and me
Rap about going in a tent
Rap about something bent.

Rap about your favourite art
Rap about your friend's cart
Rap about a school pen
Rap about your secret den.

Rap about the big long pole
Rap about the black mole
Rap about a bald man
Rap about your old Gran.

Rap about your dinner bowl
Rap about a great big hole
Rap about a spade to dig
Rap about a pink pig.

Nichol Oak-Smith (8)
Cloudside Junior School

TODDLER

Dummy dropper
Party pooper
Bogey picker
Thumb sucker
Teddy snuggler
Toy smasher
Knee bumper
Mess maker

Ashley Brooks (10) & Shannon Bailey (11)
Cloudside Junior School

BECAUSE I SAID SO!

My teacher says, 'Sit on your bottom.'
'Why?'
'Because I said so.'
'Why?'
'Because that's what I want you to do.'
'Why?'
'Because erm . . .'
'Why?'
'Because you are the only one doing that!'
'Why?'
'Why don't you stop saying why?'
'What!'

Demi Salt (9)
Firbeck Primary School

THE DOGABUNNY

What is white?
What has long ears?
The Dogabunny, the Dogabunny,
Very, very funny.

What is small and ugly?
What eats meat and veg?
The Dogabunny, the Dogabunny,
Very, very funny.

What is a puppy?
What is a bunny?
The Dogabunny, the Dogabunny,
Very, very funny.

What sleeps in a hutch?
What sleeps in a basket?
The Dogabunny, the Dogabunny,
Very, very funny.

What barks?
What sniffs?
The Dogabunny, the Dogabunny,
Very, very funny.

What's a terrier?
What's a lop?
The Dogabunny, the Dogabunny,
Very, very funny.

What bites?
What scratches?
The Dogabunny, the Dogabunny,
Very, very funny.

The Dogabunny!

Melike Berker (10)
Firbeck Primary School

OUR WORLD

The sky is blue,
The grass is green,
Together they make a lovely scene.
Life was born of all different kinds,
Each one of them had their own sort of minds.
We have now brought this world to life,
The intelligence helped us make the fork and knife.
Diseases spread across the seas,
To give an illness to flowers and trees.
Things will now rot away because of these,
But cures have been discovered like herbs off the trees.

The forests are cut,
The seas are brown,
Each one of us has a very big frown.
Hunters set off to kill the life,
Not a good use we made of the fork and knife.
Pollution was made at the same time as the cars,
Each one of them rode on the tar.
We have spoilt our world every day and night,
It's like we and the Earth have had a big fight.
We are sorry, all the time we have been in a trance,
If only we had another chance.

Christian Voce (9)
Firbeck Primary School

MY FRIENDS

My friends are good
My friends are kind
My friends are cool like you and me.

My friends are glad
My friends are lovely
My friends are kindhearted like you and me.

My friends are nice
My friends are helpful
My friends are sympathetic like you and me.

My friends are thoughtful
My friends are friendly
My friends are considerate like you and me.

My friends are unselfish
My friends are neighbourly
My friends are good-natured like you and me.

My friends are loving
My friends are not mardey
My friends are special like you and me.

Michael Charles (9)
Firbeck Primary School

SADNESS

It's very sad that lots of people died.
Soldiers are dying, enemies are killing.
People are sad on 11th of November
Try and remember and say
          Do not forget.

Gary Charles (11)
Firbeck Primary School

POPPY DAY

R   emember on 11th November
E   veryone who died
M   isery everywhere
E   very woman crying
M   emory of people who suffered
B   rave soldiers
R   ed blood all over
A   rmistice day
N   o more war
C   ry for people who died
E   mpty feeling

D   eath
A   ching heart
Y   ou must remember.

Reema Khalid (10)
Firbeck Primary School

MY FAMILY IS THE BEST

My family is the best,
Why, because I can play outside on my scooter
Because my mum and dad take me shopping
Because we buy clothes
Because we buy cookies.
My mum and dad are really kind.
My mum and dad are fantastic
I love my mum and dad like a real mum and dad.

Chloe Robinson (9)
Firbeck Primary School

WAR!

Watch all the soldiers marching away
Think they're going away for a day.
Bang, bang, bang, went the guns
While the soldiers are eating buns.

They dress in green
To camouflage the scene
All the soldiers hands are floury
When they fill in their diary.

Both the teams have a truce
While they are drinking juice
Now please remember
The 11th of November.

Sam Watson (11)
Firbeck Primary School

MY MUM AND DAD

My mum and dad wake me in the morning
My mum and dad frown with a warning
My mum and dad make me a shower
My mum and dad have love power
My mum and dad make my tea
My mum and dad take me to sea
My mum and dad comb my hair
My mum and dad are very fair
My mum and dad cuddle me tight
My mum and dad say goodnight.

Elizabeth Storey (8)
Firbeck Primary School

ALL ABOUT ME

I am prettier than a butterfly with bright, colourful wings.
I am kinder than my mum with her sweet voice.
I am stronger than my dad with his big muscles.
I am bigger than a building reaching up to the sky.
I am neater than my sister with her sweet smelling hair.
I am cleverer than a pig rolling in the mud.
I am quieter than a door when the door is closing.
I am sweeter than a sweet with its tasty taste.
I am faster than a car with its engine so oily.
I am quiet when I am asleep
But that is what Mum loves most.

Chloe Merrin (8)
Firbeck Primary School

MY MUM AND DAD

My mum and dad make my coffee
My mum and dad make my toffee
My mum and dad have lots of money
My mum and dad have lots of honey
My mum and dad live in a house
My mum and dad have a pet mouse.
My mum and dad have some ham
My mum and dad have some jam tarts
My mum and dad have a hawk
My mum and dad have some pork.

Jamahl Singh (8)
Firbeck Primary School

I HAVE A FLOWER AS BIG AS A TOWER

I have a flower as big as a tower
I only have an hour to climb it
And see what is around
I jump onto a petal
That is smooth and comfy
The smell is lovely and sweet
And the view is *wow!*
As it gets dark I fall asleep
The very next morning
I wake up in my bedroom
And it was all a dream.

Melissa Cobb (10)
Firbeck Primary School

MY BIG SISTER

My big sister
I dare not kiss her
She helps me onto my bike
But that's what I like.

She's kind and gentle
In a way
She's like a petal
That's what I say.

I love my sister ever so much
She really has a gentle touch.

Conor Roberts (9)
Firbeck Primary School

I SAW A DOLPHIN

I saw a dolphin, he looked sad
I looked again and he looked mad.
I tried to cheer him up
With a bit of a joke
And it didn't work and gave me a poke.
The dolphin was happy, clappy and jumped in the sea
With a bit of pea soup for his tea.

Nichelle Simpson (9)
Firbeck Primary School

THE ATMOSPHERE

The exosphere is 900 km above Earth
The thermosphere is 450 km above Earth
The mesosphere is 80 km above Earth
The stratosphere is 50 km above Earth
The ozone layer is 30 km above Earth
Together they make the atmosphere that
Measures 3030 km.

David Schneider (10)
Firbeck Primary School

DRAGONS

Dragons are fierce
Because they breathe fire.
Men in armour is their desire.
If they breathe fire it will be
Your pain, because fire is not a heavenly desire.
Fire burns! Burns! Burns!

Liam Blunt (10)
Firbeck Primary School

WINTER

At last the year ends once again.
The time has come to play games,
Snow fighting, making, and dreaming that you were an angel.
You settle down next to the fire with a blanket over you
Which you cuddle in and snuggle to keep you warm.

An hour later you go back out again
Crunch! Crunch!
Go your feet again and again.

You come back in again to settle yourself for something
You mix the important ingredients, sugar, spice to make everything
taste nice.
Sit down with a cup of hot chocolate, take a sip, it drains down your
body to keep you warm.

The sun comes out the snow melts away
You always feel this way and wished this day had never come.
Days, weeks and months passed since then
Again the time has come, another year has gone.

Aieza Naveed (10)
Firbeck Primary School

MUSIC IS FOR EVERYONE

Music, music in the air
Music, music is everywhere
Clap your hands and stamp your feet
Music, music, is a beat
Music, music I can't eat
Music is for everyone!

Sasha Hawkes (10)
Firbeck Primary School

MY FRIENDS

My friends are funny like a goblin
My friends are pretty like a princess
My friends like reading books and poems
My friends are kind
My friends are fun
My friends like going swimming like you and me
My friends are keen, my friends are kind
My friends like playing with you and me.

Jillian Charles (9)
Firbeck Primary School

HEAVEN

Heaven is nice
Nice and bright
White as snow
The wind will blow
When you die
I will cry
When you died
I said bye.

Liam Devine (11)
Firbeck Primary School

THE HOLIDAY

I had lots of money
To go somewhere sunny
But I had to plot
Where it was hot.
I'd feel bad to the bone
If I went alone
So in the end
I brought a friend.

Daniel Lynch (10)
Firbeck Primary School

WHEN I GO TO THE SEASIDE

Splash went the waves
When Granny tried to swim.

Splat goes the ice cream
When baby knocked it off its cone.

Squirt went the suncream,
As it hit the palms of my hands.

That's my day at the beach.

Taymar Watson (10)
Firbeck Primary School

GUY FAWKES

On the 5th of November
We've got to remember
The thirty-six barrels of gunpowder
The police went under the Houses of Parliament
And found Guy Fawkes which started an argument.
They couldn't find the rest,
So that made them the best.
And from that day on we've got to
Remember the 5th of November.

Abigail Boatman (10)
Firbeck Primary School

ANIMALS!

Horses and ponies have very bad habits
The same as little bunny rabbits.
Some kick and some fight
But the really naughty ones bite.

Hamsters are really, really small
Well they're not very tall
They're really, really cuddly
And very, very snuggly.

Laura Sanders (10)
Firbeck Primary School

MY DREAM ABOUT DOLPHINS

Dolphins, dolphins, I'm dreaming of
They're all around, I'm thinking of
Dolphins that are winking at me
Time to meet the deep blue sea.

They squeak, they peek,
Through any hole.
They can even do a forward roll.

Danielle Salt (11)
Firbeck Primary School

MY HOCKEY POEM

My hockey stick
It is the colour of gun metal
Blue and dark ruby red
With the word *Slazenger* in big bold letters.

My hockey stick
Has been battered and bruised,
It has been by my side
Through sun and rain, hail and snow.

As I fly down the left wing
With the round orange ball just by my feet
Then a cross into the middle and 'Goal!'
The ball is slammed into the back of the net.

Matthew Proctor (10)
Grosvenor School

ELF

Trees reach the sky,
Like eager hands.
The moon looks down
Like a big eye.

Creatures lie in wait,
Still like logs.
They wait for
The wood elves to dance.

All know the spell,
The fair folk cast,
The danger is never told,
For all are entranced.

White and purple swirls,
Precede the magic.
The light feet tap,
Like gentle rain.

Golden hair swishes,
Like a swirling sea.
Soft singing floats
Filling the air with good.

When the dance stops
When the good has gone,
I put down my book,
The story has ended.

Lucy Parkinson (10)
Grosvenor School

GARETH GATES

Gareth is a superstar,
He is the best by far.
I love the way he has his hair,
I can't help but stand and stare.
He is cute and neat,
He is just so sweet.
Gareth is a superstar,
He is the best by far.

Gareth is a superstar,
He is the best by far.
The words he sings I think are great,
But not liked by my sister Kate.
I love the joy he brings along,
With his brilliant songs.
Gareth is a superstar,
He is the best by far.

Hannah Litchfield (9)
Grosvenor School

MY FRIEND

I have a friend who is quite small
But in my heart he's very tall.

He's been my friend since I was born
If I lost him I would be torn.

We do not like to be apart
And when I go away he comes
With me to play.

I bet you wonder who could be so big
It's my best friend Wibbly Pig.

Jack Chambers (9)
Grosvenor School

SUMMER

Summer is a time for happiness,
Summer is a time for fun,
Summer is a time to laugh and sing,
Summer is for everyone.

Summer is a time to swim in the sea,
Summer is a time to dance with glee,
Summer is a time to never frown,
Summer is for everyone.

Summer is a time to rest in the sand,
Summer is a time to always be glad,
Summer is a time for love and care,
Summer is for everyone.

Helen Oshinusi (11)
Grosvenor School

THE CATS

I found a black cat and a fat cat
Running silently through the mist
Making no sound except for a *pssst*.

Walking in mid-air no one would know they were there
Surrounded by thin air but they don't care.

I found a mad cat and a sad cat
Both looking at the bridge
Playing with the small green midge
But I don't think they should be playing there
Because they might fall off the steep ridge.

Emma Kenworthy (9)
Grosvenor School

ROBOT WARS

Crashing and smashing fighting machines
The robots are in the arena
Battering with spikes and slicing with blades
Bits of metal go flying in the air
Wire and batteries litter the floor
A robot is dead.

The house robots come in for their fun
To trash and bash and burn and crunch
The arena has secret surprises
Grinders and flippers and air jets.
The robot gets cooked in a flame pit
It burns.

A house robot is in for a big surprise
Sir Killalot is attacked by Razor
He snaps the chain and makes Killalot stop
He chews on Sgt. Bash's chainsaw motor
Dead Metal slices Razor, Matilda flips him
The house robots win!

Christopher Threadgold (9)
Grosvenor School

A POEM FOR MUMMY

Roses are colourful
Roses are beautiful
Roses are fragrant
Roses are always there in my garden
Roses remind me of you
And I love them just like you.

Rachel Waring (9)
Grosvenor School

AN AUTUMN NIGHT

The howling wind blew over the field,
As darkness approached an autumn night.
As poppies swayed, squirrels played,
Oh what a wonderful sight!

Small barn owls starting to wake,
Silence and emptiness in the sky.
Rabbits scattered over the field,
With the moon rising high.

The corn waving in the field,
Mud everywhere on the ground.
And people's conversations,
Drown the blackbird's sound.

People shouting in the market,
Church bells ring out loud and clear,
Laughing from all the school children,
As men in the pub have a pint of beer.

The shops in the village are closing now,
The day is getting on.
Children's lights are going off,
As another day is gone.

As the day ends noise starts to rise,
As discos start and rough boys fight.
The howling wind blew over the field,
As darkness approached an autumn night.

Hollie Mulligan (11)
Grosvenor School

A Trip To Aberdeen

One, two, three
We all took the ferry
Four, five, six
Me, Julia, Tom and Mrs Beex
Seven, eight, nine
It was just fine
Ten, eleven, twelve
We made fun of ourselves
Thirteen, fourteen, fifteen
We visit the Castle of Aberdeen
Sixteen, seventeen, eighteen
Tom got lost, he was only thirteen
Nineteen, twenty and twenty-one
Mrs Beex was upside down
Twenty-two, three and four
She fell unconscious on the floor
Twenty-five, nine, thirty
And a lady with a baby
Thirty-one, two, three
They bring us back to the ferry
Thirty-four, five, six
Me Julia and Mrs Beex.

Alienor Prokopowicz (9)
Grosvenor School

TOAD'S NEW SUIT

There was once an old toad all slimy and brown,
who needed a new suit to go into town.
He went along to see his friend water rat,
who lived in a hole that belonged to a bat.
Water rat said, 'I know what you'll like
so jump on the back of my two-seater bike.'
They cycled down the road to see tailor frog,
who had opened a new shop next door to the bog.
Toad tried on a jacket made from wings of a fairy
and then a bat skin, which made him look scary.
Clothes on, clothes off, clothes on, clothes off
whatever toad wore made tailor frog scoff.
'With your fat body nothing will fit you,' said
water rat who could see toad in a stew.
Frog had an idea and went out to the back
of his shop where he kept a rubbish sack.
With some snips of his scissors, the clips of some pins
And the sticking of labels taken off tins.
When he had finished and come back into the shop,
What toad saw made him hop and hop.
A cloak fit for a king along with a crown
And off toad went to have fun in town.

Charles Gotts (9)
Grosvenor School

FUN IN THE SUN

We went to the Caribbean on our holiday
We flew out on a Saturday.
The hotel looked over a beautiful bay.
My parents wanted to swim in the sea
But that wasn't for me.
The pool looked nice
And I was in there in a trice.

Hungry I got, I had a Caribbean tea
Which was just right for me.
So it was time for goodnight.
Tomorrow I would swim with my might.
The next day I caught a fish.
I cooked it and had it for lunch
That was quite a dish!

Gabriella Stephenson (9)
Grosvenor School

SUNFLOWERS

Sunflowers - they are so tall,
Reaching up the garden wall,
Yellow petals facing the sun,
Admired so much by everyone.

Bees visit every hour,
Collecting pollen, like yellow flour,
Leaves so green I have not seen,
A thing so lovely in my dreams.

Olivia Harrison (10)
Grosvenor School

BARN OWLS

Barn owls are different shades of brown and white,
They're quite nice and covered in soft feathers.

They have blue feathers on the tips of their long wings,
They put twigs and other things in their nests.

Two or one baby chicks are born each year
They are born without hair from their tail to their ear.

The barn owls like to fly at night
Because of their very sharp eyesight.

They fly up then swoop down
To catch their prey for food.

I like barn owls, I think they're cool,
In my bedroom I can hear them hoot and hoot.

Ben Harker (10)
Grosvenor School

THE BIRDS

The birds sing their song early in the morning,
So everybody thinks what they're eating,
The birds are singing for all the day,
So everybody has a perfect day,
At the evening everybody goes sleeping,
So the wonderful birds stop singing,
It will be the same for tomorrow.

Catherine Foisy (10)
Grosvenor School

HAIR CAN . . .

Hair can be straight
Hair can be curly
Hair can be boyish
Or even quite girly.

Hair can be blonde
Hair can be brown
Hair can be tied up
But I like it down.

Hair can be horrid
Hair can be nice
Hair can be pretty
And a good home for lice!

Mary Earps (9)
Grosvenor School

GREMLINS

Gremlins they come out at night,
Gremlins their colours are bright,
Gremlins they love to fight,
Gremlins they feed on blood,
Gremlins they live in the mud,
Gremlins their eyes are green,
Gremlins make sure they're not seen,
Gremlins make a mess in my room,
'Quick Mum will be back soon!'

Joe Egglenton (9)
Grosvenor School

MY VALENTINE

My valentine is nice
My valentine is cute
My valentine is the best in the world.

My valentine is smart
My valentine is clever
My valentine helps me with my work.

My valentine is helpful
My valentine is kind
My valentine is very nice to me.

I don't know how to talk to my valentine
I don't know how to speak to my valentine
But I know how to love my valentine.

Sarah Morley (11)
Grosvenor School

A KITTEN'S FAVOURITE POSITION IS . . .

A kitten's favourite position is sitting on the floor
with its tail curled round,
Or maybe lying on a patio, enjoying the sun's warm rays,
It could be stretched out in a basket, asleep,
But I think that it's in front of a food bowl,
polishing off every last scrap,
That's a kitten's favourite position.

Nicholas Powell (9)
Grosvenor School

MY BEST BAND - BUSTED

Busted have just become stars
And I think they *will* definitely go far,
From the day since their career
They have been great from that first year.
Their names are Matt, Charlie and James,
I love them all the same,
I think they're great in every way,
So what else can I really say,
Apart from that they will be my best band always.

Anna Bradley (9)
Grosvenor School

SNOW

Snow, snow so light,
Snow, snow so white.

Snow falls everywhere from the sky,
Oh how it just likes to fly.

Snow, snow so cold,
Snow, snow so bold.

I look into it at night,
And see that it is really bright.

Snow, snow it melts in the sun,
And that means no more fun!

George Farraj (9)
Grosvenor School

RICHARD'S BAD LUCK!

Richard of York,
ate lots of pork,
until one day
he started to snort.

His wife was scared,
and almost despaired,
so she stopped cooking pork,
because she cared.

His neighbours looked away,
and he stopped going out in the day,
the dog was his only friend,
Richard was full of dismay.

At long last Richard got better,
he went for a walk with his red setter,
when he got home
he had received a letter.

It was offering him a job,
with a man named Bob,
It was in a new town, starting next week,
his wife was so happy she started to sob.

They packed up their house,
including the pet mouse,
the job in Liverpool was great,
and they even learnt to speak scouse.

Then one day his wife cooked duck,
by the end of the week he had started to cluck,
it was happening again,
what terrible bad luck!

Thomas Vickerstaff (10)
Grosvenor School

THE BEAUTIFUL HOUSE

This is the beautiful house
It was owned by Mr Douse
But it was too much for him
He said the garden was too slim.

When the wallpaper was white
He said it was too bright
When the sofa was black
He said it should be moved back.

When the staircase was wood
He said it never should
Have been there
He said it was very rare.

When he went to the opticians
There were suspicions
That he was blind as a bat
Then he realised that.

He realised that the house was beautiful
He felt so tearful
The wallpaper was white
But not too bright.

This is the beautiful house
It was owned by Mr Douse
It was too good for him
And the garden was not too thin.

Jack Dickie (10)
Grosvenor School

AUTUMN IS . . .

Autumn is a golden season
I press my cheek against the window.

Then I hear a hunter nearby
Then I hear a deer die.

Autumn has a colour clash
Then I see my teacher dash.

Autumn is a hunting season
Hunters have lots of gunpowder and
treason.

Rabbits hop, dogs bark
Blue tits twit and eagles hark.

All the leaves blow off trees
Including the bees.

Charlie Scott (10)
Grosvenor School

THE CRAFTY VIXEN

By the light of the moon I saw a shadow of the sly vixen,
her cubs she had to feed, so with heed,
she sniffed round the chicken pen,
she saw a gap and slid through the crack and into the chicken's run.
Up to the door she did slither, the chickens heard her, they did quiver.
With her nose she nudged up the door, sitting there she was sure,
a big fat hen with eyes on storks,
no more eggs would the fat hen lay as this was her final day.
With one fatal swoop the hen was dead,
the vixen carried it off without its head.
Down the field to the set she did run to feed her cubs, the job was done.

Charles Shortland (11)
Grosvenor School

THE START

When I was one
I had just begun.

When I was two
I learned to use the loo.

When I was three
I tried a cup of tea.

When I was four
I walked into the door.

When I was five
I learnt to dive.

When I was six
I learnt to pic 'n' mix.

When I was seven
I lived in Heaven.

When I was eight
I stood at the gate.

When I was nine
I learnt the time.

When I was ten
I got a new pen.

When I got to eleven
I hope I'm not in Heaven.

Ross Whiting (10)
Grosvenor School

AUTUMN

The wind blows through a field of corn
Whistling past their ears
Ready for them to be picked at dawn
With autumn's well known shears.

The apple orchard is filled with a sweet smell
Of ripe fruit swaying in the breeze,
You can hear the song bells
Singing in the trees.

Winter's coming soon,
Better get wrapped up warm,
At night you can see the moon
And whipping winds could get you torn.

Ellika Larsson (10)
Grosvenor School

WEATHER

Pitter-patter on the windowpane
Oh no it's raining again.

The trees sway in the breeze,
Along with the rustle of leaves.

The icy gusts are hard to fight
As they blow with all their might.

The sun comes out and shines so bright,
And brightens the world till day is night.

Alex Brown (10)
Grosvenor School

MY MOUNTAINS

Way up high, can you see?
Mountains stand strong and tall
Where people can freely ski
In the snow which softly falls.

Rising up into the sky
The weather can be fierce too
Listen I can hear them sigh
Looking down on you.

I feel so free high up there,
The wind wraps itself around me
Looking down on valleys so fair
Watching people and trees.

I really miss my mountains
For a minute I'm in a trance
Skiing on my mountains
High up there in France!

Elizabeth Harper (10)
Grosvenor School

THE SEASON'S CIRCLE

It all starts at spring
Where we all begin to sing.

Summer then appears
Where school is at the rear.

Autumn is the beginning of cold
This is a season for silent and old.

Winter is the end of it all
But then it is all recalled.

Samuel Robinson (10)
Grosvenor School

WHEN I WENT TO THE ZOO

I went to the zoo
And saw a kangaroo
It jumped so high
It nearly reached the sky.

Second I saw a monkey
It seemed to be looking at me
Swinging from tree to tree
How happy it seemed to be!

Then I saw a giraffe,
It made me laugh
What a long neck it had
The giraffe looked so sad.

Next I saw a snake
It scared me and I started to shake
It slithered onto a rock
I'm glad the cage had a lock.

Last I saw a lion
It looked so strong as if made of iron
This was an incredible thing
That's why it's the jungle king.

I walked to the car
Home isn't very far
Home at last
The day went so fast.

Tucked up in bed
I rested my weary head
Dreaming of things you can do
When you're at a zoo.

Sam Buxton (10)
Grosvenor School

THE GUESSING GAME

I live in a cupboard under the stairs
In a rectangular box with my two friends.

What am I?
I am what.

I'm composed very tightly to enemies Jim and Susan,
I hate their netted circles as they give me bumps and bruises.

What am I?
I am what.

I'm taken outside in podgy grips
To be thrown into then harshly hit.

What am I?
I am what.

I see colours yellows, reds and greens,
As I zoom through the air at a terrific sound.

What am I?
I am what.

Crowds gasp as I sail towards the ground
Then they all cheer producing a great level of sound.

What am I?
I am what.

At the end of the day, when the sky turns red,
I'm pressed against clothes and I go to bed.

What am I?
A tennis ball of course!

Alexandra Hearth (10)
Grosvenor School

A BALL'S LIFE

It's dark in the bag
With a soggy old rag,
My emotions are rapidly elated
As a hole is quickly created.

A blast of bright light,
It must be at night
As I'm gripped tight
And given a fright.

I'm out on the pitch
Then in a muddy old ditch
As a foot reaches back
And gives me a whack.

I soar in the air
And land I don't know where,
Then I'm feeling all wet
As my back hits the net.

The whistle sounds loud,
There's a roar from the crowd,
Then I'm back in the bag
With a soggy old rag.

Jonathan Lister (10)
Grosvenor School

THE MOOOOON! POP!

A silvery light,
Hung in the sky,
It came down from Heaven,
And shone down on Devon,
And, Presto! the cows could fly.

The cows that could fly,
Leapt into the sky,
And found that the light of the moon,
Turned their tummies to jelly,
And gave them green wellies,
Then inflated them like a balloon.

They drifted away,
And landed one day,
In the car park of the 'Cat and the Fiddle,'
They stopped for a half,
And the bar man just laughed,
As they popped like bubbles on hay.

Ian Welch (10)
Grosvenor School

WEATHER

Sun feels like an oven cooking you for life
Snow is icing sugar covering the world
Snowmen are like ornaments
Frost is sugar candy but it turns into slush
Wind is a hurricane whirling through the sky
Rain goes slitter spatter on the windowpane
Hail is like boulders falling from the sky
Fog is thick wallpaper that never stops.

Liam Carroll (8)
Keyworth Primary & Nursery School

136

FAVOURITE WEATHER

Whining whooshy wind
The wind swishes
It makes a slight breeze
Rain spits and splashes
Snow like icing sugar
Falling from the sky
Frost is like a freezer
Hail hits down on you
From the sky
Fog puts cars out of control
Lightning strikes
Flashes and crashes.

Ethan Moult (7)
Keyworth Primary & Nursery School

A HOP, SKIP AND A JUMP

We jump along
We jump in time
We jump for luck
We jump in line
We jump up high
We jump in twos
We jump for joy
We jump in queues
Sometimes we just need to jump
Just a hop, a skip and a jump!

Hannah Reilly (9)
Keyworth Primary & Nursery School

SUMMER HOLIDAY

Summer holiday is the best time of year
No moaning teachers, no boring lessons
Just time to chill out here.

In France the sun always seems to shine hot
Time to make new friends, places to see
French food is brill, I eat the lot.

But the summer holiday soon seems to end
New shoes, new pencils, lots for Mum to spend
It's good to be back, to see my friends.

Sarah Robins (9)
Keyworth Primary & Nursery School

UNTITLED

Wind is wild
Wind is a breeze
Wind whispers
Wind settles down
Wind wrecks
Wind wrecks
Wind costs lives
Wind dries the washing
Wind chases leaves
Wind dies down.

Jacob Sjenitzer (7)
Keyworth Primary & Nursery School

MY TEDDY

My favourite teddy
I cuddle him when I'm scared,
His name is Freddy,
Because I don't care!

People take the Michael out of me,
Because his name is Freddy,
Just let them be,
Because I don't care!

People take the Michael out of me,
Because he is green,
Just let them be,
Because I don't care!

Me and my teddy,
We don't care,
Because his name is Freddy
He is my favourite bear!

Evie Clegg (7)
Keyworth Primary & Nursery School

WEATHER FORECAST

The sun is the sweet of our lives
Wind ruffles your hair like a wild beast
Raindrops like a dolphin
Raising into the air
Storms stopping you going outdoors
Hail hurts
Mist and fog
Hard to see through.

Ellie Snooks (8)
Keyworth Primary & Nursery School

SILENT WORLD

S ound gives us inspiration
O r maybe it's stupid!
U nless you say
N o it's important
D eaf people understand.

B elieve me
R ealise something
I t's quite obvious
N o sound creates loneliness
G one is a gift taken for granted
S ilence is all around.

H oping to remove it
A bility to hear
P erhaps never occurs
P ossibly
I t is a hope
N othingness
E veryone communicates
S imply by laughter
S ound brings happiness to our world.

Thomas Burrows (7)
Keyworth Primary & Nursery School

WEATHER

Sun shiny
Hotter than a fried egg
Storm horrible, shaking down trees
Snow is fun to play in
Make good snowballs
Wind cold
Blows the washing off the line

Luke Woolley (8)
Keyworth Primary & Nursery School

WEATHER

Lightning wrecks trees
Lightning flashing in the sky
Lightning costs money
Lightning costs lives
Lightning wreck sheds
Lightning like a sharp knife
Lightning wakes people in the night,
Scary.

Edward Welham (7)
Keyworth Primary & Nursery School

THE ANGEL

He came with the dawn.
On Monday he gave needed food and medicine to the
starving people of the world.
On Tuesday he fed and clothed the desperate refugees
as they fled from the terror of their homeland.
On Wednesday he evaporated all cars and lorries and
instead gave people bicycles.
On Thursday he freed all captured animals and put a
stop to poaching so animals could live in safety.
On Friday he took away all weapons and taught people
to care for one another.
On Saturday he cleansed the air, land and sea so they
were safe to live in.
On Sunday he shared out his gift of hope.
So everyone could at least hope that the bad times would end.
So that peace, love and goodwill could prevail over evil.
He left at twilight.
As he disappeared into the night, he murmured,
'Now have another try.'

Katie Taylor (11)
Nottingham Girls' High School

LOVE

I met at dawn the Princess of Love
She was so gentle
Her pet was a white dove
And she smelt of sweet menthol.

She wore a dress of pink
And a cloak of white
Which at the back had a kink
She was as beautiful as the night.

Her sandals were cream
Her nails were pink
She had hair as blonde as a dream
She made you think.

She lived in a pink heart
Her eyes were warm and soft.
Her lips were as red as a jam tart,
It was if she was floating aloft.

I left her that night
Forever thinking of her bright
And beautiful sight.

Emily Oliver (10)
Nottingham Girls' High School

THE FROG PRINCESS

She came with the waterfall.

On Monday,
She made all plants green and lush
As if they had been painted over with a new layer.

On Tuesday,
She made sure that all orphanages
Had queues of people just dying to adopt a homeless child.

On Wednesday,
She made all scientists and doctors have brainwaves
So that every ill person could be cured.

On Thursday,
She made all crops grow
Into lovely food.

On Friday,
She turned all shacks into beautiful little cottages
So that every ill person would have a warm place
To sleep at night.

On Saturday,
She flew all animals in captivity back to their natural habitats
So that they could be with their families.

On Sunday,
She made everyone loving and caring, but
She was so tired, and did not reach the other realm.

She left with the lake, and she flew with a gust of wind.

She whispered to the whole wide world,
'Now have another try!'

Jess Engler (10)
Nottingham Girls' High School

CAVEMAN!

When our teacher brought in a caveman,
It created quite a riot,
'Cause the caveman attacked the teacher
And the class wasn't at all quiet.

The caveman whacked him on his ear,
The caveman whacked him on his nose,
The teacher hopped right round the classroom,
Crying, 'Ouch! Oh, my toes!'

Here's a lesson to all teachers -
Don't create a riot,
'Cause when the caveman finished with the teacher,
The class wasn't at all quiet!

Rebecca Donaldson (10)
Nottingham Girls' High School

BLUE SNOWMAN

Please don't judge by what you see,
Take some time to find the real me.
Not the one who stands silent by the foot of a tree,
The me that wishes to be free.
Free from a prison full of winter and ice,
Into a world that seems . . . nice!
With lush green fields and a blue starlit sky,
And my own snowman igloo on a mountain up high.
Where I can relax in a bath of warm foam
That is the place I'd like to call home.

Daisy Gudmunsen (11)
Nottingham Girls' High School

ANGER

A flaming footstep burns the ground
In the valley dark and deep.
A deep-throated bellow tears the sky
As anger wakens from his sleep.

Terrifying birds fly through the sky
That's shrouded in smoke and gloom.
As the predators of the ground stalk the valley
In the darkness and poisonous fume.

His fiery eyes burn red
As he stalks his hunting ground.
The hunting dogs come
At the horrible baying sound.

Rachel Kenny (11)
Nottingham Girls' High School

WHY AM I SO SPECIAL?

My mummy thinks I'm special
As pretty as can be.
My daddy says I'm funny
There's no one quite like me!
I love to go to bed
But only for a while,
I soon creep back down again
With such a cheeky smile!
My sisters think I'm naughty
I 'borrow' all the time
Well why not I say
When everything is *'Mine!'*

Kate Selwyn (10)
Nottingham Girls' High School

IMAGINARY WORLDS

A rolling sea, blue and sparkling,
A desert with nothing but sands,
A mountain of snow, cold and windy,
A picture from one of these lands.

A dream, flaring faintly,
A fuzzing spinning daze,
A daydream in a whirling world
An aura in a misty haze.

A daydream in my sleepy mind
Dazzling inspiration hard to find,
A spark of something - pshh! It's gone!
All the fun is left behind.

Who creates them, why are they made?
Why is it sleep in which they are laid?

You're just there - then you're

    Falling,

        Falling,

            Falling . . .

And it's

Gone.

Elly Gladman (10)
Nottingham Girls' High School

WATER

I once noticed a tiny stream
Which glistened like a bright sunbeam
It lay near a mountain summit
Which caused a gentle downward plummet.

It dances and prances through a lair unknown
It tinkles and sprinkles to make music of its own.

It springs and flings that humble stream
It glisters but whispers of the wonders it has seen

It glides and slides, stealthy and unknown
It flows and gently goes under rock and under stone

I once noticed a flowing river
The pure water made me shiver
I knew where that river flowed from
The stream that from my mind had gone

It rushes and gushes through a cluster of trees
It whirls and swirls against the breeze

It swishes and wishes it could give joy
It waves and slaves to one very small boy

I once noticed a downwards plummet
Which started from a majestic summit
This wonder was a waterfall
From the stream I'd known when I was small.

It thunders and wonders when the fall will end
It crashes and bashes in the downward descend

It spouts and shouts the route to the seas
It smashes and crashes the froth that it breathes

All this came from a tiny stream
Which glistened like a bright sunbeam.
It lay near a mountain summit
Which caused a gentle downward plummet.

Anna Redgate (11)
Nottingham Girls' High School

THE HAUNTING

She came one night,
Hair raven-black,
Whistling in the wind.
Her eyes red with fury,
Unfinished work,
In her head revenge pinned.

What had she come for?
Why had she come?
For the murder of her son!
She came one night,
Hair raven-black,
She had worked as hard as a nun!

She came one night,
Hair raven-black,
Whistling in the wind.
She took away the soul,
Of the man who stole her son,
Whistling in the wind.

Nidhi Sahdev (11)
Nottingham Girls' High School

NATURE

Nature comes in many forms
Like deserts, lakes and woods
Rain and shine and winds and storms
Are its many different moods.

The animals that live there
Love their habitat.
From tiny ants to a big grey bear
From a monkey to a cat.

And when the sun has finally set
More animals come out
Whether their place is cold or wet
They're still slinking about.

Rebecca Brown (10)
Nottingham Girls' High School

THE WORLD IS A DREAM

The world is a dream,
A dream to live in,
A dream that will last for some time,
Everybody's dream is different
Like a snowflake they aren't identical
The world should be treated like life,
When happiness is about
The world is a beauty
We should appreciate this life
And make it worth living
For a dream doesn't last forever.

Sophia Ali (11)
Nottingham Girls' High School

A Jungle World

Monkeys chatter in the tops of trees,
Swinging on the branches with the bend of their knees.

Hippos splashing in puddles of mud,
Leopards falling off trees with a *thud!*

Parrots squawking overhead,
Baby crocodiles going to bed.

Oranges falling off the branches of trees,
Little elephants eating their teas.

Huge wild boars are stamping the ground,
Sleeping tortoises are safe and sound.

Sophie Reeve (10)
Nottingham Girls' High School

Lady In White

She walked softly by the dark blue river,
With bare feet, a white gown and long black hair.
She walked and she never gave a shiver,
She walks along without a single care.
She moves gracefully and she never slips,
She comes to walk every single night.
Her body is very tall with pursed lips,
She is in a trance while she is walking,
She always walks slowly with a straight back.
She is always silent never talking
As if in her life some happiness did lack,
When she is walking the birds start squawking,
When she is here she never starts talking.

Rosie Lenaghan (10)
Nottingham Girls' High School

LOVE

I met at dawn the Queen of Love
Her eyes were warm and blue,
On her shoulder stands a dove
And her feet bear no shoes.
Her hair was as orange
As the sunset sky,
So long and luscious
The dream never dies.
Her dress is pure white
In folds of silk,
Right down to her feet
As white as milk.
Her victims enchanted
By her spell of Love.
Lives of confused emotions
Lives like Heaven above.
I met at dawn, the Queen of love
Her eyes were warm and blue.
On her shoulder stands a dove
And her feet bear no shoes.

Jessica Moses (11)
Nottingham Girls' High School

THE MAN FROM SPACE

There was an old woman from Perth,
Whose husband had just come to Earth.
He'd been to eat planets,
And comets of granite,
Now it's six thousand miles round his girth!

Megan Holmes (10)
Nottingham Girls' High School

FISHES

Fishes are long.
Fishes are fat.
Fishes are short.
Fishes are flat.
Fishes are pink.
Fishes are green.
Fishes are dirty.
Fishes are clean.
Fishes are big.
Fishes are small.
Fishes can be any,
Shape, size or colour at all.

Ebele Egbuna-Ruiz (11)
Nottingham Girls' High School

ANGER

I met at twelve (the vampires' hour)
One whose face was dripping with blood;
He then approached the phantom tower -
Cold and grey he pulled up his hood.

His cloak was dark and reached the ground
His eyes were red and bloodshot
He looked about in the shadows nowhere to be found
Breathing rapidly he took out his pot.

He then gulped down the contents within
And seemed to get stronger.
He sprinted into the dead of night;
But tomorrow eve he will be back much longer.

Beware of the vampire he's hungry . . .

Abigail Packham (11)
Nottingham Girls' High School

SPACE KENNING

Moon, stars,
Venus, Mars,
Sun, sinks
Saturn's, rings,
Velvet, blue,
Clouds out too,
Solar system
Far and distant,
Galaxies, comet,
Astronauts vomit,
Milky Ways,
Sun rays,
Winds subtle,
Space shuttle,
It's all a race
In *Outer Space!*

Sonali Chandi (10)
Nottingham Girls' High School

FRIEND OR ENEMY?

My friend is most of the time friendly,
Kind, generous and sweet,
But then sometimes she turns into a big, nasty,
Ferocious, quite scary monster.
She growls and howls and sometimes even barks.
She mumbles and grumbles and has a face like a bull,
And then turns back to normal again.
She leaves me with this decision to make,
Is she good or bad?
But more importantly is she my *friend or enemy?*

Georgina Robertson (10)
Nottingham Girls' High School

GODDESS OF SADNESS

I met at dawn the goddess of sadness
Who emerged from the trees.
Her eyes were dark like the glistening stream,
Which faded under the moon in peace.

Her hair was like the darkening sky
Which conquered the light clouds like ballet.
Her ghostly face crept among
The lifeless saddened valley.

Whispers of laughter once forgotten
Danced over lands without slowing.
The goddess' heart was forlorn,
And the misty darkness was glowing.

Her lips were deathly droplets of blood
Which streamed over mountains high.
Her dress was blue of silky tears,
Amongst echoes of a lonely cry.

Jasmin Evans (10)
Nottingham Girls' High School

ANGER

I met at dawn, the Devil of Anger
He had a red and raging face,
He carried on him a sharp metal dagger,
Danger in a haunted place.

His clothes were dull and red,
About his head were devil's horns,
And a glowing red bump above his forehead,
After every breath was a long pause.

His size 12 feet wore big red boots,
His legs were covered in hair,
Around him were tremendous hoots,
But it's the Devil of Anger, he doesn't care.

I met at dawn, the Devil of Anger,
He had a red and raging face,
He carried on him a sharp metal dagger,
Danger in a haunted place.

Annie Hud (10)
Nottingham Girls' High School

THE LORD OF ANGER

I have seen him many times, the Lord of Anger
His eyes glint fiery red.
When he passes things wilt and die,
He wishes that everything was dead.

Around his head is a ring of flame
His cape is dark, his face mundane
He is surely the terror of the land
But in his rage he is somehow sad.

So if you see the Lord of Anger
Hide and let him pass
And when he's gone we'll sing a song
'Let our holy peace last.'

Helen Poulson (11)
Nottingham Girls' High School

MY DOG

Cat chaser
Good racer
Wet nose
Good pose
Black knight
No frights
Record breaker
Friend maker
Good kicker
Excellent licker
A dog
Not a frog!

Catherine Rhodes-Jones (10)
Nottingham Girls' High School

MIDNIGHT

At midnight the shining moon comes out in the dark and
misty sky,
At midnight the prowling wolf comes out into the woods
and howls in the moonlight,
At midnight the lamp posts come on to guide people's way
round the roads,
At midnight the owls come out and sit on the branches of
the tall swaying trees in the wind,
At midnight cars come up their steep drives from the party
they have been to,
At midnight you can see all the lights turn off as people go
to bed,
At midnight all the curtains are pulled and everyone is now
asleep.

Shhhhhhhhhhhhhh!

Jessica Crooks (10)
Nottingham Girls' High School

—

SNOOZE

My cat Snooze,
Likes chewing the fuse,
That connects to the wire,
It could start a fire!

Alice Conlin (10)
Nottingham Girls' High School

HOMEWORK

Homework, homework on my bedroom floor
Homework, homework on the bathroom door,
Homework, homework down the loo
What on earth am I going to do?

I hate homework it is mean
My bedroom's never clean
Full of homework every day
What else can I say?

Homework, homework down the drain
Homework, homework in my *brain!*

Stacie Butler (10)
Robin Hood Junior School

THE SNOW

Snow snow you melt all over me,
Snow as cold as ice,
Why don't you melt, answer me?
Sometimes you're as cold to stick to my fingers
You turn ice cubes,
Cubes that are frozen in the morning,
But dissolve in the night,
But when you're gone you're back again,
Snow snow that's all I can say,
Snow snow go away
But please snow come back another day.

Daniel Marshall (11)
Robin Hood Junior School

MY FAVOURITE SEEMS TO BE . . .

Chocolate, chocolate,
I love you!
Yummy yum!

I need chocolate, night and day!
Because of your sweet taste.
Because you're creamy and full of luscious caramel.

My favourite seems to be . . .
Let me have a think . . .
My favourite is . . .

Ah yes . . .
No! That's not it.
Ahhh, white chocolate.

My favourite seems to be . . .
White chocolate,
Milk chocolate.

My favourite seems to be . . .
Hmmmm
I don't know!

Kimberley Brown (10)
Robin Hood Junior School

DIEGO FORLAN

Diego Forlan, Diego Forlan
Running down the footie pitch
He kicks the ball for all he's worth
And it lands in the back of the net.

Sam Bramley (10)
Robin Hood Junior School

WHALES AND DOLPHINS

W ater and wind
H ow they jump over the waves
A shark with evil, evil eyes
L ive till the others die
E vil sharks every day
S hrimps as the dolphins eat them.

A lways nasty as he swims around
N ervous dolphins and whales
D eep blue sea water.

D on't they look pretty
O n the top of the sea
L oving little creatures
P ut your soft hands on me
H aving fun with us, but
I nstead of the people
N obody comes anymore
S ad and lonely.

Natalie Garner (11)
Robin Hood Junior School

THE GHOSTS

Justin and Jamie went up the mountain to fetch a ghost called Tom.
Then Jamie fell down and broke his neck
Then Justin came tumbling after.
Then Tom, Justin and Jamie's soul went round scaring people
Forever after.

Steven Higgins (11)
Robin Hood Junior School

GOD'S HANDS

'My love will protect you!'
God told the sleeping fox
And I'll never forget that evil the scarlet dawn beheld.

The sunlit sky was golden with heat!
God was staring at the inhuman people with their bloodthirsty
swords
And the hounds tearing at the flesh the fox (the dear fox) owned.

The screeching of agony scared the wild animals in their habitats
And dolphins wailed and stopped leaping out of the water,
Happily they frowned and water trickled down their eyes,
The oak trees swayed sorrowfully.

Then time froze and a gold staircase appeared,
The fox with its curiosity climbed the holy stairs
And time was natural again.
He waved to his cubs and vixen.

'Don't cry or worry, for I have no pain
Also I'm in good hands, I'm in God's hands.

Zoë-Maria Wright (11)
Robin Hood Junior School

THE COCOA CHOCOLATE!

Take a big bubbly bite,
Feel it all squishy and mounting,
Melting in your mouth,
It is extremely exciting,
I wish it could last as long as I live,
But it melts as quickly as a snowman.

Ashley Warsop (11)
Robin Hood Junior School

THE DRAGON KING

Dangerous and strong, tough as dynamite.
The biggest and very mean.
The baddest and thickest-skinned.
Claws as sharp as metal knives.
Fire breath as hot as lava.
So watch your back.
Stay on guard.
Watch out it's the dragon king!
He is using his wings
To call a tornado to attack our city!
Watch out he's using his fire breath to try
And burn our city to the ground!
Let's squirt him with water!
Swoosh goes the water!
Yay! He's gone for good!

Mark Thornton (11)
Robin Hood Junior School

DOLPHINS

	D	ark blue and grey dolphins
H	O	pping through the water
	L	aughing with each other
S	P	lash, splash, splash playing
	H	ide-and-seek
Gr	I	nning dolphins
	N	ervous baby calves
	S	ilver silky skin.

Chantelle Brown (10)
Robin Hood Junior School

The Mad Tortoise

There was a mad tortoise named Trish
Who wished for a satellite dish
So she took off her shell
And rang the bell to try and get a satellite dish.

She looked everywhere
But only found a pear
Sitting on the sofa chair.

She got an idea
And used her pear
Until she didn't need it anymore
But used her shell as a satellite dish.

Katie Ley (10)
Robin Hood Junior School

Robin Hood

Rabbit, rabbit spinning round and round.
Octopus, octopus making a wiggly sound.
Bird, bird eating lemon curd.
Iguana, iguana in the race came third.
Newt, newt having fun, chasing a big tasty bun.

Hawk, hawk flying as fast as a bee,
Owl, owl who's fantastic at teasing me.
Ostrich, ostrich who is very, very proud
Duck, duck who is really loud.

Sean Duryea (10)
Robin Hood Junior School

THE JUNGLE POEM

Lions go *roar roar roar*
Snakes go *hiss hiss hiss*
Monkeys go *who e who ah ah*
And their throws are a total miss.

Parrots squawk in trees
Mosquitoes nest with bees
On the bright green leaves.

Eagles fly above
With the hawk and the dove
A sound of a dragon goes *uh uh uh.*

Nathan Watson (10)
Robin Hood Junior School

SUMMER IS MY FAVOURITE TIME OF THE YEAR

Summer is my favourite time of the year
With the blue shiny sea and the burning sun shining upon you.
The green grass waving to and fro.
The flowers jumping up and down around you.
Summer is my favourite time of the year
When everyone is happy and joyful.
Summer is my favourite time of the year
When animals, people dancing on the sand.
Summer is my favourite time of the year.

Sadie Duryea (10)
Robin Hood Junior School

COOKIES

I love cookies
I love cookies
I bet you can tell that
I love cookies.

Sometimes I eat them after dinner
Sometimes I eat them after lunch
Sometimes I eat them in the morning
Sometimes I eat them in a bunch.

I love cookies
I love cookies
I bet you can tell that
I love cookies.

Sometimes I take them to school
Sometimes I take them to my mamas.
Sometimes I take them to my friends,
Sometimes I take them to my nanas.

I love cookies
I love cookies
I bet you can tell that
I love cookies.

Jemma Ward (11)
Robin Hood Junior School

AUTUMN LEAVES

Autumn autumn everywhere
Leaves curling down to our hair
Brown leaves yellow leaves it does not care
Autumn here
That's what we are meant to talk about.

Rhys Donaghy (11)
Robin Hood Junior School

WINTER

Winter is freezing cold and makes me shiver loudly
Winter is funny when you throw crunchy white snow at people
Splat!
Winter is frosty, the grass crunches loudly.

Ryan Bush (10)
Robin Hood Junior School

SNAILS

S   is for slippy slimy tracks
N   is for noisy shell
A   is for angry shell
I   is for being ignored
L   is for being last
S   is for always being slow.
     So
     What are we?

Amanda Broughton (11)
Robin Hood Junior School

WINTER

Winter is cold wind blowing gently in the air
Winter is freezing ice crackling loudly on the ground
Winter is fun snowballs melting in your hand.

Thomas Teer (10)
Robin Hood Junior School

WINTER

Winter is icy ground evaporating slowly
Up into the air.
Winter is windy air, floating quickly through my hair.
Winter is snow falling quickly on my roof.

Martha Finch-Bretlaender (10)
Robin Hood Junior School

IN THE JUNGLE

In the jungle you will see
Monkeys twinging from tree to tree,
Now you see them now you don't
You might get killed but maybe you won't.

Trees are swaying in the night
The tigers may give you a horrible fright,
In the terrifying jungle of the night.

Lewis Smith (10)
Robin Hood Junior School

WINTER

Winter is cold and blowing hard on the window
Winter is freezing ice melting fast on the pond
Winter is windy air blowing softly everywhere.

Kimberley Foster (9)
Robin Hood Junior School

SPRING, SUMMER, AUTUMN, WINTER

Lush green leaves on the oak tree,
Fluffy white lambs in the meadow,
Wonderfully warm Saturdays with your grandma
Spring, summer, autumn, winter.

Summer, autumn, winter, spring
An aqua blue sea sopping the sand
Vanilla ice creams with hundreds and thousands
Opaline clouds and a forget-me-not sky
Summer, autumn, winter, spring.

Autumn, winter, spring, summer
Gold, brown and orange leaves floating down,
Steaming hot cocoas after sundown,
Children's laughter as they prance in the snow,
Autumn, winter, spring, summer.

Winter, spring, summer, autumn
Sparkling white snow on the ground,
Jolly snowman in every garden,
Snowball fights in the evening,
Spring, summer, autumn, winter.

Kim Chalk
Robin Hood Junior School

WINTER

Winter is icy snowflakes falling peacefully on the hard floor
Winter is cold snowmen melting slowly in my back garden
Winter is windy weather blowing noisily outside.

Nicole Linford (9)
Robin Hood Junior School

WINTER

Winter is breezy, windy quickly everywhere
Winter is freezing cold, damp on the ground
Winter is frosty ice, rock solid on my car.

Jake Garner (9)
Robin Hood Junior School

WINTER IS . . .

Winter is ice breaking up in pieces
Underneath your feet.

Winter is freezing snowflakes dancing
Slowly in the air.

Winter is cold wind blowing quickly
Round my ear.

This is what I think winter really is.

Charlotte Undy (10)
Robin Hood Junior School

WINTER

Winter is freezing and crackling on the icy floor.
Winter is snowy and falling quickly on the ground.
Winter is windy and freezing on a bare frosty tree!

Jade Spencer (10)
Robin Hood Junior School

WINTER IS ...

Winter is slippery ice melting on the ground
Winter is windy weather blowing against your head
Winter is frost melting on the gate.

Jendayi Davis (9)
Robin Hood Junior School

WINTER IS ...

Winter is precious, small flakes
Falling on my jewelled grass.

Winter is cool ice running
Glittering on my legs.

Winter is frost frosting
Upon my windowpane.

Jodie Hamilton (10)
Robin Hood Junior School

WINTER

Winter is frosty snow trickling softly on the trees.
Winter is breezy ice melting slowly on the road.
Winter is cold wind blowing quickly everyone.

Samantha Shephard (9)
Robin Hood Junior School

WINTER

Winter is snow melting quickly on the ground.
Winter is ice crackling peacefully on the pond.
Winter is wind blowing softly in the trees.

Billie Waines (10)
Robin Hood Junior School

WINTER

Winter is snow melting
Winter is cool snow freezing
Winter is precious ice melting snow.
Winter is falling snowflakes on my face.
Winter is cold.
Winter is ice.

Jordan Plummer (9)
Robin Hood Junior School

WINTER

Winter is slippery ice melting slowly on the road
Winter is freezing air blowing furiously in my face
Winter is snowflakes falling quickly through the window.

Leon Parsons (10)
Robin Hood Junior School

IMAGINATION

If I had the chance I would touch a freezing icicle
while it talks to another.
I wish I could smell a hot-coated fur tiger
under a dead leaf tree.
I would like to smell horses' hooves galloping by the riverside.
I wish I could hear a dripping sugary icicle dripping
by the startling sun.
If I had the chance I'd touch the roar of a lion when it chases
its dinner.
I would like to feel the squeak of a mouse as it scrapes at its cage.
I would like to hear the scales of a dragon as it spits fire from its mouth.
If I had the chance to smell the splash of a dolphin as it flips
into the bubbly ocean.
I wish I could feel the sun's sharp golden rose.
I wish I could touch a cooking fish going help! Help!
While the chef tosses and turns it on the barbecue.

Abigail Colgan (9)
St Edmund Campion RC Primary School

NEVER TRUE

I wish I could fly and touch the morning sky.
I wish I could paint gravity flowing through the air.
I wish that cartoons would come to life right in front of my eyes.
I wish I could fly with a magic carpet through a waterfall
And let the glittering water drop on me
But everyone knows that will never be true.

Simon Krawczynski (9)
St Edmund Campion RC Primary School

IMAGINATION

I wish I could see the flowing air that travels all around us
I would like to hear the fishes' song
I want to dance with the coloured insects
as they hop, skip and jump through fields.

I wish I could feel the birds' wings flap gracefully in the wind.
I would like to glide on an eagle's back as it dives through the clouds.
I want to paint the wind as it blows around the world.
I wish I could run across the lava that stands in a volcano
as it turns the crusty rocks.
I would like to walk on water like I walk on the ground.
I wish I could stop a bomb and save millions of lives.

Alice Whitehouse (10)
St Edmund Campion RC Primary School

AN IMPOSSIBLE WISH

I wish I could see the sun in the sky
I wish I could be the fish in the sea
I wish I could be the God in the world
I wish I could be the sunshine in the sky
And make people happy
I wish I could be the person in your dreams
To save you when you have a bad dream.

Eve Miller (10)
St Edmund Campion RC Primary School

IMPOSSIBLE POEMS

I wish I could paint the howl of a wolf as it settles on the full moon
And hear the lion's roar in the waves of the sea.

If I had the chance I would like to draw the smell of a flower
As it sways in the breeze,
And I wish I could fly with the eagle across the mountains and snow.

I would like to see a robin's song in the morning's dew
And I wish I could smell a tree breathing in the pine forests.

If I had the chance I would hear a root of a plant
Singing in the undergrowth,
And watch wild horses as they sail with the clouds.

Hatty Clark (10)
St Edmund Campion RC Primary School

IMPOSSIBLE

I wish I could hear a freezing icicle as it freezes in the cold.
If I had the chance I would catch the tears of the moon
as they fall from the night sky.
I wish I could hold the stars in my hand as they
spin in the night sky.
If I had the chance I would paint the lion in the sun
as he roars.
I wish I could hold the world in my hand as it spins.
If I had the chance I would cook the sea in a pan.

Luke O'Brien (9)
St Edmund Campion RC Primary School

IMAGINATION

I would like to paint the roar of dinosaur as it rumbles through
the jungle.
I would like to hear the horn of a unicorn while it gallops
across the sea.
I wish I could hear a plant grow as it's in the field.
If I had the chance I would like to hear an icicle talk while
it sits in the blazing sun.
I wish I could fry the night sky in a frying pan.
I would like to hear the scales of a dragon as it flies
through the open air.
I wish I could paint the sound of a horse galloping across
the open plains.
I wish I could touch the monkeys swinging from tree to tree
in the moonlight.
I wish I could fly the open air with eagle's wings.
I wish I could touch a cooking fish as it shines through the sea.
I wish I could draw the sound of horses in the morning.

Danny Leech (9)
St Edmund Campion RC Primary School

IMPOSSIBLE

I wish I could see a unicorn in the winter snow.
I wish I saw a fish flying over a waterfall.
I wish I saw a dog on the moon
And I wish people could live forever and ever.
But of course I'd like to see with my eyes closed.
And out of all the things I've said,
I'd love to fly in the midnight sky.

Jack Stratton (9)
St Edmund Campion RC Primary School

IMAGINE IF . . .

Imagine . . .
Imagine if I could hear the smell of steaming water in the
snowy mountains.
I would like to draw the sound of a flourishing dog running
through the grassy fields.
I wish I could paint the feel of a gritty rock in the desert sand.
Imagine if I could smell hazy windows in the rain.
I would like to hear the smell of cooking chicken on a
warm summer's day.

I wish I could hear the feel of the rusty bark on a tree.
Imagine if I could feel the smell of calming lavenders in the garden.
If I had the chance I would touch the sound of a thunderstorm
in the brightness of the moon.

Uzo Oforka (9)
St Edmund Campion RC Primary School

IMPOSSIBLE

I wish I could ride on the back of a flying horse
as it soars over cities and mountains.

I would love to sit on the back of an eagle
as it soars over freezing forests and towns
swooping and swerving looking for prey.

I wish I could feel the sound of a volcano as it erupts.

George Phillips (9)
St Edmund Campion RC Primary School

IMAGINATION

If I had the chance I would like to touch
an everlasting cloud.
I wish I could touch one thousand phases as
they were floating around the sky.
I would like to touch an invisible elephant.

I wish I could paint one thousand paintings all in one
on a ship sailing across the world.
If I had the chance I would paint the smell of a
cooking fish sailing across the seven seas.
I would like to paint a glue stick gluing all its paper
in the middle of the ocean.

If I had the chance I would like to hear paintings whisper
to each other.
I would like to hear a freezing icicle in the middle of a desert.
I wish I could hear a book read out its pages.
I would like to smell a painting of a wonderful big orange.
I wish I could smell some eagles flying through the sky.

Katherine Busby (9)
St Edmund Campion RC Primary School

IMAGINATION

I would like to paint the sound of music booming out of a stereo.
I wish I could hear the water flap up against the shore when I am
in school.
If I had the chance I would hear a plant stretch and grow to be
as tall as a dragon on its hind legs.
I would like to paint a tiger's roar as it tries to kill its small prey.
I wish that when I was painting the walls I didn't spill paint.

Joe McLaughlin (9)
St Edmund Campion RC Primary School

THE TREE BEAST

How would one describe the tree beast?
Elusive, strange and rare.
It's bigger than a forest cat
But smaller than a bear.

Its arms are long and waving
They number two times two
Its favourite food is rats and mice
On their bones it will chew.

Its fur can change to background
Like the scaly creep chameleon
Its range of colours number
Over sixty thousand billion!

From its slender shoulders, burst slimy, scaly wings,
The voice box lets it make very high-pitched pings.

But man is very quickly using up the world's supply
So the kind and furry tree beast is doomed to sadly die.

Patrick Liddle (9)
St Edmund Campion RC Primary School

IMAGINE

If I had a chance I would peel off the scales of a dragon
As it soars through the deep blue sea.
I wish I could see a headless chicken run around as it pecks
the food off the ground.
I would like to blow the writing off a piece of paper.
If I had a chance I would lift up the smell of a dog.
I wish I could lick the smell of chocolate.

Philippa Killingworth (9)
St Edmund Campion RC Primary School

IMAGINATION

I wish I could hear the sun's spine creak
I would like to feel a skunk fly over New York City
in the window.
I wish I could see a monkey with my nose while it's
playing football.

I would like to lie on a black cloud while it's
flying over Australia,
I would like to hear a pair of false teeth talk,
I wish I could smell a leprechaun's beard.

I would like to see a tree turn inside out while growing,
I wish I could feel the sun's tears while it's shining.

Tom Collins (9)
St Edmund Campion RC Primary School

I WOULD LIKE TO . . .

I would like to paint an eagle's wings as it flies through
the cold and open air.
I would like to feel horses galloping through the meadow,
I would like to lay on a dragon's back as it breathes fire.
I would like to hear flowers whispering to each other.
I would like to see monkeys painting the moonlight.
I would like to paint the smell of a skunk.
I would like to see a chicken pecking at the seeds with no head.
I would like to see a baby goat running with no legs or feet.

Ella Lunn (9)
St Edmund Campion RC Primary School

IMAGINATION

I would like to paint the roar of a lion
as it dozes in his den.
I wish I could hear burning on a cold, chilly day.
I would like to smell an icicle landing on the blazing sun.
I wish I could feel a flower growing taller than me
on a rainy day.
I would like to smell a snake slither through the grass.
I would like to paint the scales of a crocodile as it
swims through the muddy water.
I wish I could hear a waterfall on top of me.
I wish I could see what life really is like for my friends.

Losarina Kelly (10)
St Edmund Campion RC Primary School

I WISH

I wish I could watch horses galloping across the oceans
While wicked witches stirred up their potions.
As I sat upon the rock there was no sound of a clippity clock.
I would like to paint the air they had passed
While all of them stormed off in a mighty blast.
They were going at seventy miles an hour
Using up all their strength and power.
Off they went in such a hurry
Just the way that a skunk would scurry.
It wasn't like going across the fields
Among the calm and gentle breeze.

Jennifer Hendron (9)
St Edmund Campion RC Primary School

IF ONLY . . .

If only I could feel the sound of the waves
as dolphins jump through them.

I wish I could ride a butterfly,
through heated jungles afar.

I would like to paint the screech of an eagle
as it soars over mountains.

If I had the chance I would hear the smell of a flower,
from a valley far away.

If only I could draw the sound of horses' hooves,
galloping over dry plains.

I wish I could stroke a lion,
prowling after an antelope.

I would like to watch frost creep over a tree,
in the middle of a frozen night.

If I had the chance, I would paint the song of a robin,
as it hops in the morning dew.

If only I could see the sound of a wolf,
as it howls endlessly at the moon.

Elena Cahill (9)
St Edmund Campion RC Primary School

IMPOSSIBLE POEMS

In the morning dew sparkling!
I wish I could feel horses hooves galloping across
the shining waters!
In the night sky!
I would like to touch the lion's roar in the midnight sky!
In the woods!
I wish I could paint the howl of the wolf in the moonlit woods!
Flying away!
I wish I could fly with the eagle following the never ending sky!
In the sea!
I wish I could paint the splash of a dolphin!

Amelia Mara Kildear (10)
St Edmund Campion RC Primary School

IMAGINATION

I wish I could hear a lion roar as it
snoozed on the long, thick, painted grass.
I wish I could see an eagle as it approached the
sunset night.
I wish I could touch the splashes of a dolphin
as it jumps into the sunset sea.
I wish I could touch a freezing, snowy, icy mountain.
I wish I could hear a panda as it leapt through the painted forest.
I wish I could hear a horse galloping in a dewy spring morning.

Nicole Fleming (9)
St Edmund Campion RC Primary School

SPACE

I've always wanted to go into space,
I've seen it in books and it's a great place,
Great shiny stars of fire and heat
Bumping into everything that they meet.
But I like the planets, they're wonderful things,
Great big balls of gas with colourful rings.

What fascinates me most about the Milky Way
Is the planet Pluto which is dark in the day.
No stars has Pluto, no colours or moons,
It's not like a real place, like in cartoons
It's hard to think that a girl just eleven years old
Named this planet, or so I'm told!

And the sun is just so amazing like a big yellow flower,
Blasting out its heat, showing off its power,
The sun is hot and full of light
Shining out rays bringing a moon to the night.

So now you can see why I want to go to space,
Because it's such a fabulous place!

Emer Pearson (10)
St Edmund Campion RC Primary School

PLUTO

Pluto is as small as a pompom ball
Pluto is as purple as Jupiter
Pluto is as round as a football
Pluto is as small as an ant
Pluto is as purple as an octopus
Pluto is as round as the moon
Pluto is as cold as ice.

Andrew Hodgson (8)
St Edmund Campion RC Primary School

IF I WAS A LITTLE WHITE SNOWMAN

If I was a little white snowman
I'd skid across the ice
I'd go and see the icy cold hens
And look at ice-cold mice.
I'd dive in deep, cold waters
And try to walk to foreign lands
I'd try to make myself have hands
But sadly I could not.
But playing in the snow is cool
But I'd really like to see the sand
But sadly I could not
Because I'm going away . . .

I'm gone . . .

Maria Brennan (8)
St Edmund Campion RC Primary School

THE SUN

The sun is a lemon without the juice
It is fire without the sparks
The sun is an orange without skin
It is lava without the flow
The sun is a light bulb without electricity
It is a sunflower without the petals
The sun is a ball without the stripes
It is a planet without ice
The sun is a meatball without the taste
It is man without the name.

Radha Nehra (9)
St Edmund Campion RC Primary School

THE ANGRY MOB

The angry mob that lives next door,
They're rotten bullies and horrid to the core,
I asked Bill, I asked Bob,
Who's the angry mob
That lives next door?

Bob replied and so did Bill,
Down my spine it sent a chill,
'The angry mob is none other than
Jim Jam, Jill Jam and Tim Tam.'

I did say Tim's mad,
But what was it that sent them bad?
Maybe it was sardines, maybe it was milk,
Maybe it's their basket lined with linen and silk.

This is the saddest life a cat could live,
I'll spend the rest of it in a garbage bin,
For my dearest friends are the angry mob.
Who live next door.

David Ayland (8)
St Edmund Campion RC Primary School

THE COUNTRYSIDE

See the birds in the clear blue sky,
Hear the birds soaring through the air,
The trees, swaying from side to side,
The leaves making everything nice and colourful.
The flowers making the colour come to life.
The plants that fill the Earth with joy.
This is what makes the beautiful countryside.

Ellen Newsome (8)
St Edmund Campion RC Primary School

OH FIDDLESTICKS

Whenever something goes wrong
Something is lost or something not done
Someone's too late or taking too long
Oh fiddlesticks, where's that gone?

Teachers have to be patient all day
'You have to be perfect,' she'll say
But sometimes things don't work out that way
Oh fiddlesticks, what did I say?

Get on with your work, try your best
Please don't spoil it for the rest
I've lost my glasses, oh what a pest
Oh fiddlesticks, whatever next.

Elsa Esberger (9)
St Edmund Campion RC Primary School

THE SUN

The sun without a ball
It is a yellow bouncy ball without its bounce
The sun without electricity
It is a lemon without its juice
The sun without coldness
It is Saturn without its ring
The sun without movement
It is a football without its spring
The sun without water
It is a balloon without the burst.

Géiléis Garrett (9)
St Edmund Campion RC Primary School

SNOW

When the snow is falling
All over town
I put on my gloves and shoes
As the snow goes down and down.

I go outside to the great outdoors
Throwing snowballs at my friend
We go down the garden path
And turn around the bend.

The snow is great fun
I love the snow
But the bad thing is
It soon has to go.

I see the snow falling down
So I build a snowman
Then I put on eyes and ears
And then I call him Ben.

James Laverty (10)
St Edmund Campion RC Primary School

PLUTO

Pluto is a grape without its juice
It is like a ball without air
Pluto is like some blackcurrant without water
It is a marble without glass
Pluto is a pancake without colour
It is a football without stripes
Pluto is very, very, very, very, very cold
Very cold . . .

Joseph Saczek (9)
St Edmund Campion RC Primary School

SPACE

Space
It's such a wonderful place
The Milky Way
Takes my breath away
Jupiter, Saturn and Mars
And don't forget all those stars.

Now I'm going to my rocket with Vicki
And I think it's getting a bit nippy
How far away
Is space today?
I wondered hard and bright.

Then we went home
My mum gave a groan
She said, 'Where have you been?'
I answered, 'I've been to space,
The wonderful, dark, and scary place.'

Alice Colaluca (10)
St Edmund Campion RC Primary School

MY HAMSTER

My hamster's gone green
His nose is as big as a cow
You would faint if you saw
Him dance, jump and bow.

My hamster's eyes have gone pink
They're popping out its head
He never stops to blink
And never goes to bed.

Lucy Moore (9)
St Edmund Campion RC Primary School

THE BOOKWORM BLUES

Join the Bookworms, do it now!
You'll like this book and you'll say
Wow!
So come with me to castles far or
explosions planted in a car.
And travel to exotic lands and join
up with the marching band.
Whether you're a boy or a little girl
a good strong book is sure to hurl
you into the darkest bits of space
or to a secret agent base so read a
book that suits your taste
If you do not you're a big *disgrace!*
So come on in and join this chant
Don't ever, ever say you can't
Yeah!

William Flynn & Patrick Liddel (9)
St Edmund Campion RC Primary School

VENUS

Venus is like an apple without the stalk.
Venus is like a grape without the juice.
Venus is like a ball without the bounce.
Venus is like a marble without the glass.
Venus is like Uranus without the rings.
Venus is like the Earth without the blue.
Venus is like a helmet without the strap.
Venus is like a kiwi without the hairs.

Ruth Bentley (8)
St Edmund Campion RC Primary School

STARS IN SPACE

Twinkle twinkle little star
I wonder how far up you are?
Floating in the dark
I love to watch you from the park.
Twinkle, twinkle little star
I wonder how far up you are?
All the stars
Surround Mars
Go to Earth
For a new star has come to birth
Twinkle, twinkle little star
I wonder how far up you are?

Niall Voice (10)
St Edmund Campion RC Primary School

MARS IS . . .

Mars is a button without the holes
It is a ball without the bounce
Mars is the sun without the yellow
It is like a cola can without the cola
Mars is a mountain without the point
It is a feather without the fluff
Mars is lead without the pencil
It is an apple without the skin
Mars is a pen without the ink
It is a badge without the pin.

Lila Bird (8)
St Edmund Campion RC Primary School

RAIN, RAIN

When I woke up this morning
I couldn't stop a-yawning
I went over to the windowpane
And to my surprise I saw some rain
It came down like frogs
Or cats and dogs
The rain formed puddles
That looked like huddles.

It was all so very scary
To survive in that you'd have to be a fairy
I looked down the lane
But oh no just more rain
Quickly I got bored
But at last I'm reassured
Tomorrow will be a sunny day
I hope I pray.

Connor Rowden (11)
St Edmund Campion RC Primary School

WEATHER

W ind howling all around, leaves swirling all around.
E arthquakes rumbling and crumbling all the Earth.
A sunny day rose for the first time this year with a
   shocking beam of light.
T hunder arose the dirty black sky with a mighty flash.
H ail crashing on people's heads making them a little red.
E very evening it darkens the whole city bringing it a little
   nippy.
R ain clouds coming our way bringing a little stay in our day.

Catherine O'Reilly (10)
St Edmund Campion RC Primary School

SPACE, SPACE

Space, space, that incredible place, silent
and spooky without a trace of life.
The only way in is by rocket, when you are going,
you cannot stop it!

The movement of stars and the glowing of Mars.
Neptune is very blowy whilst Pluto is very snowy!
Mercury is the opposite so incredibly hot!

That is not a lot compared to Venus,
(which is 482° centigrade)
Earth is our home planet, sadly it is badly
spoiled by many forms of pollution
including oils.

Edward Stuttard (10)
St Edmund Campion RC Primary School

THROUGH THE WINDOW

I woke up this morning on the wrong side of bed,
Where I couldn't help my yawning and I was horrified with dread.

I looked through my window to see what was there
The rain was pouring and the trees were all bare.

Later that morning as I looked through again
The songbirds were singing and whistling through the wind.

The sun was setting and the rain had stopped,
The animals came out but the owls did not.

Declan Holland (10)
St Edmund Campion RC Primary School

THROUGH THE WINDOW

It's raining, raining, raining bad
Raining, raining, really mad
Every morning it's really dull,
The rain starts like a raging bull.

I want to go outside and start playing
Instead of just lying
It's really, really heavy
Please, please stop this raining.

The rain, the rain it never stops
The rain, the rain, it's boring and dark.
Rain, rain that is all it does
It never stops raining mad.

Vicki Henry (10)
St Edmund Campion RC Primary School

WEATHER

W eather that's what this is about,
E   very bit the weather changes,
A   bit of rain and thunder lightning,
T   hat's what the weather is,
H   owever my favourite weather is the snow,
E   very day different kinds of weather come and go,
R   ain, thunder, lightning, sun, snow they're not that
bad after all.

Katrina Crosby (10)
St Edmund Campion RC Primary School

A SPACE OF DARKNESS

The movement is only orbiting
In the stillness of a pitch-black space
Travelling slowly
Going quickly
Moving at their own pace.
Brightness of colour mixed with black
In a truly silent world.
Making the planets seem even
More beautiful
In a twirling, swirling whirl.
The stars glimmer lifelessly
But always, always there
Making the space seem simple,
Nothing to make it care.

Helen McPake (11)
St Edmund Campion RC Primary School

PLUTO

Pluto, a cold ice cube
It is as big as a skyscraper
Pluto, as round as a football
It is as strong as a metal door
Pluto, a lonely planet
It is a long, long, long time away,
A long time away . . .

Bryn Pryse-Jones (9)
St Edmund Campion RC Primary School

SPACE!

In outer space
Beyond the stars
As I pass Jupiter and Mars
What a venture
It would be
If all the world
Could only see
What I see now
Through my own eyes
All the wonders
Of the skies!

Lauren Kelly (11)
St Edmund Campion RC Primary School

SPACE

I was in a fantastically huge spaceship
I really had to have a pace.

I saw every planet and I really had to have it
Aboard this ship there is no tip.

My telescope is a thing to handle
It's as big as million candles.

We got so close to planets left
It almost had to be a theft.

Andrea Rollini (10)
St Edmund Campion RC Primary School

SPACE TRAVEL

Through the atmosphere
Up into space
Going to another planet
A brand new place.

Look through the window
A scene I love so much
There's the Milky Way
Is it close enough to touch?

Out of the spaceship
Into deep space
There's a pattern of stars
As intricate as lace.

We're heading towards a distant star
A glowing ball of light
Hangs there in the blackness
Of the eternal night.

There's planets moving around that star
Like flies around a light
There's one with a big hole in
The scar of a great fight.

I step onto the planet
Wobbling at first
Not a drop of water there
I'm building up a thirst.

I lie down on the surface
There's a light breeze
There's a funny smell down here as well
Now I know, it's *cheese!*

Jenny Booker (11)
St Edmund Campion RC Primary School

SPINNING THROUGH SPACE

In the centre burning bright
Is the sun, a ball of light
Always day never night.

Spinning, twirling
Hurling, furling
Are the massive planets.

The universe is black kms of dark
With huge gas planets that spin in arcs
But on only one does life play and lark.

Spinning, twirling
Hurling, furling
Are the massive planets.

Earth, Venus and Neptune blue
Jupiter, Uranus and Saturn too
Mercury, Pluto, Mars old not new.

Spinning, twirling
Hurling, furling
Are the massive planets.

I'm spinning through space
On a race against time
My heart's thudding every time.

Spinning, twirling
Hurling, furling
Are the massive planets.

A comet's coming, I'm hiding in bed
Mixed feelings rush through my head
This time tomorrow I could be dead.

Spinning, twirling
Hurling, furling
Bang! Goes my planet.

Helena Lee (10)
St Edmund Campion RC Primary School

WEATHER!

I stared out of my window,
What could I see?
Floods and floods of rain turning to sea,
Why when it's raining is it so cold?
In other places it never rains or so
I've been told.

Street lights gleaming in the night,
Small and glowing balls of light.
Still it's pouring down with rain,
Darkness is now taking over the
light,
Better go to bed now,
Au revoir, bon soir, goodnight!

Sophie McGowan (10)
St Edmund Campion RC Primary School

ALIENS!

Aliens were travelling
Through space vast,
And they seemed to be travelling very fast,
Their first destination was Planet Spon,
But in a flash they were gone.
Next they went to Planet Groo,
But every citizen there told them to *'shoo!'*
After that they went to Planet Htrae,
Seemed like Earth but the other way.
Soon they decided to go home,
But when they got there, they were alone.

Adam Harrison (11)
St Edmund Campion RC Primary School

WEATHER

One sunny day I went out to play,
The sun was glistening in the day.

The paths were boiling because of the hot sun
And the flowers were growing tall.

The shining sun made the day long and bright
But at the end the flowers would tilt because they
had nothing to drink.

Gabi Rozwadowska (10)
St Edmund Campion RC Primary School

THROUGH THE WINDOW

It's raining outside so I'm staying in
It's dark and dull out there
But I'm bored, bored, bored, bored, bored
I'm watching the rain on the window sill going pitter-patter,
pitter-patter.

I'm getting even more bored now it's been going on for hours now
I ask Mum if I could go out and play and she says no.
I do wish it would snow, not rain.

Francesca Godden (10)
St Edmund Campion RC Primary School

RAINING

R aining raining all day
A puddle of water over there
I   n the night a drip drip comes
    from outside
N ew day put on your coat and go
    outside
I   t's damp but still sunny
N ext minute crash, flash a storm
G rowing louder and louder.

Emma Lyons (10)
St Edmund Campion RC Primary School

WEATHER

One night
I looked through the window
And saw the heavy rain
Cold and icy water against the windowpane.

A crash of thunder
Followed by a flash of lightning,
The bitter wind howled
It all seemed very frightening.

On the drive lay an old toy of mine,
As ice gripped everything it could.
It sent a chill down my spine
As I saw that silence had even
Taken the distant wood.

The next morning I hoped for sun
But as I ran to the window,
I realised there was none.

James Ayland (11)
St Edmund Campion RC Primary School

SNOW

I saw the snow on the grass
Just like a big white mass,
As the pink-faced children passed,
I dashed across the grass,
Just then I saw two children clash,
Then I said, 'When is it going to pass?'

Claire Killingworth (11)
St Edmund Campion RC Primary School

Somewhere In Our School Today . . .

It's wet break and a group of girls embarrassedly huddled
up in a corner.
The teacher, Mr Nutty Professor, slapping his hands,
madly shouting, 'Don't climb on the table
Jonathan.'
Lee was shouting, 'It's not wet play.'
Year 3 happily swing on the swings.
Class 5 and 6 skilfully playing football
shouting names out loud.
Nursery happily playing on the slide.
A group of Year 1 skilfully playing hopscotch
as well as smiling.
A bunch of Year 2 playing kiss-e-cats.

Katie Dickinson (9)
Stanstead Primary School

The Undiscovered Centaur

The undiscovered centaur was very thick and dumb
He tried to tell me something about the United kingdom.
I tried to tell him that he was wrong but he wouldn't listen
So he ran away at rapid speed.
I tried to keep up but he tripped up and started to bleed.
The courageous centaur didn't cry
He said he was all right but he told a little lie.
He turned around and guess what I found, a tag saying 'goodbye.'

Thomas Stovell & Corey McGhee (8)
Stanstead Primary School

THE ROBBER

I saw a robber go creeping, sneaking by
I saw a robber telling the police a lie
I saw a robber steal a car,
I saw a robber steal someone's chocolate bar.

I saw a robber go creeping, sneaking by
I saw a robber being very, very sly,
I saw a robber who was very quick,
I saw a robber playing a sneaky trick.

I saw a robber go creeping, sneaking by
I saw a robber poke someone in the eye
I saw a robber rob a bank
I saw a robber make someone walk the plank.

I saw a robber go creeping, sneaking by
I saw a robber making someone cry,
I saw a robber chuck someone in the sea,
I saw a robber spying on me.

If you see a robber go creeping, sneaking by,
Stay away or you will die.

Thomas Savage & Jay Jackson (9)
Stanstead Primary School

THE WITCH

There was a wicked witch, she will turn you into a toad
'I'll crush your brains' it said, on a jumper she had sown.
The wicked witch she has grey hair,
With her magic wand she will make you disappear.
She will crumple your bones and make your blood freeze
When she rides past on her broom she makes quite a breeze.

Jessica Brazener (8)
Stanstead Primary School

IN THE WITCH'S KITCHEN

In the witch's kitchen
Green and dusty,
Her black sly cat, staring up at me.
In the witch's kitchen
Her crooked broomstick hovers,
Waiting to fly.
In the witch's kitchen
There are dead rats and bloodthirsty bats.
Potions bubbling in the enormous cauldrons.
In the witch's kitchen
The witch is waiting for the
Bubbling potions to be done.

Aiesha McLaren (9)
Stanstead Primary School

IN A WITCH'S KITCHEN

In a witch's kitchen
There are black cats with big green eyes
There are fat rats with their tails cut off.
In a witch's kitchen
There is a bubbling, steamy cauldron.
There are jars all over the place.
In a witch's kitchen
There are spiders' webs dangling down
There is a wicked witch
Waiting to turn you into a frog.

Joshua O'Sullivan (9)
Stanstead Primary School

THE WITCH'S KITCHEN

The witch's kitchen is smelly
Like an old pair of shoes,
The witch's kitchen is spooky
Like a dark cave.
The witch's kitchen is dusty
Like a house not lived in for years,
The witch's kitchen is dark
Like an approaching thunderstorm.

The witch's cauldron is steamy
Like smoke coming out of a train,
The witch's kitchen is boiling
Like a blazing hot fire.
The witch's cauldron
Contains a deadly potion.

Louise Banister (8)
Stanstead Primary School

THE WITCH

Witches are not nice people at all,
They don't like children because they bawl.
Her kitchen is musty
The jars all rusty.
Eyes of rabbit, little dog tail,
If you are there, she'll turn you into a snail.
She climbs onto her wooden broom and disappears
over the moon.
    Zoom, zoom, zoom.

Sophie Liddiard (9)
Stanstead Primary School

SOMEWHERE IN OUR SCHOOL TODAY . . .

. . . A group of children distinctly swing on the apparatus
Class 5 tragically came in from play.
Six stupid second-graders spy mysteriously on the teachers.
An army of infants stamped madly around the playground.
Ten teenagers trip up tactically to tick the teachers
Twenty-two infants dawdle so that they can happily miss music.
An infant looks up at the board precariously, amazed at what he sees.
A class sadly looks at what pronouns are.
Twenty-four unhappy students grumpily put their homework
in their folders.
Etc!

Nicky Rood (9)
Stanstead Primary School

THE WITCH'S KITCHEN

It's smelly and dirty, dusty and jumbled.
A black cat guards a cabinet
Full of potions, poison and dead rats.
The air is full of flying bats
The cauldron boils and steams
Hanging from the ceiling's beams
And the red ripe apples gleam in the steam.
This is the witch's kitchen,
It has a theme of rhyming to a beam.

Kieran Booth (9)
Stanstead Primary School

SOMEWHERE IN OUR SCHOOL TODAY . . .

Class 5 are silk measuring rectangly
When teacher is standing.
When she is eating Walkers crisps and Miss Clom is sitting
When the teacher was talking
And the headteacher Mr Max came and said,
'Can I have Sam please.'

'OK . . . yes . . .' said Miss Clom.
Mr Max has got to shout at Sam.
Sam has gone out of the door.
'Sam to Mr Max's office.'
In twenty minutes Sam comes back and
Mr Max comes back and Sam is crying his eyes out.

Sam read a poem out.
Shock, shock,
under the sea
and caught a man for its tea.

Justin Scothern (10)
Stanstead Primary School

THE WICKED WITCH

When I had my dinner a wicked witch
Turned me into a toad.
My dad said, 'What's going on?'
So she turned my dad into a magpie.
She looked at the mirror and then it cracked.
A spot on her nose, she is so ugly
And smelly and she turned green.
She screamed, she screamed so loud
She fainted.

Liam Bostock (9)
Stanstead Primary School

SOMEWHERE IN OUR SCHOOL TODAY

Somewhere in our school today
Miss Higgens' class are doing footie
Miss Armstrong is nicely doing the register
Miss Wilde is doing FLS
Miss Densham is getting ready for lunch
Mr White is making a phone call
   Now it is lunchtime.

Liam Baker (9)
Stanstead Primary School

SOMEWHERE IN OUR SCHOOL

Somewhere in our school today, nursery are loudly singing
nursery rhymes and Year 5 are madly working out the times.
As soon as the class was dismissed a bunch of boys are having
a little game of football.
Three people fall over
In fact about twenty people fell over to prove it was a vital game.
The girls were just screaming their heads off round the playground.

Ricky Wootton (10)
Stanstead Primary School

SOMEWHERE IN OUR SCHOOL TODAY

Five crazy teachers are precariously pretending to be ducks.
A cluster of children have scientifically inspected the school.
A group of pens have stupidly ran out.
A silly child has fatuously put his head down the toilet.
One teacher nervously rings the firebell.
A superb poet blushes proudly as he reads his poem aloud.

Chris Wilson (9)
Stanstead Primary School

SOMEWHERE IN OUR SCHOOL TODAY

Twenty four kindergartens clumsily draw on the new curtains
Two bleeding children are sitting quietly outside the reception
nearly hurt
The Year 5 and 6 are willingly battling out a game of football.
The nursery are stupidly picking their noses till they have a nosebleed.
Nineteen silly infants are building Mount Everest with their
building bricks.
A herd of teachers ran really quickly but could not make it to the
toilet.
Etc.

Thomas Crampton (9)
Stanstead Primary School

SOMEWHERE IN OUR SCHOOL TODAY . .

Class 1 are quietly listening to a story.
Class 2 are madly drawing a picture.
Class 3 are being badly behaved.
Class 4 are boringly doing maths.
Class 5 are sadly doing work on India.
Class 6 are gloomily watching a video.
Mr White is sadly looking at his laptop.
Mrs Armstrong is madly walking around.
Miss Allison is badly running around school.
Mr Hitych is sadly jogging around his car.

Danny Wheeler (10)
Stanstead Primary School

SOMEWHERE IN OUR SCHOOL TODAY

A group of children are speedily running to the hall.
While a group of children are spectacularly acting.
Some artists are excitedly looking at the work of Paul Klee.
Twenty-four happy infants are bobbing up and down precariously.
A poet is skilfully building suspense into his poem.
A game of football is frustratingly cut short by the play time bell.
Two children are cautiously closing the glass door to the art room
Where children were continuously getting told off.
A small group of girls are stupidly making a mess
When the teacher said, 'Don't do it again.'
The headteacher is crazily shouting at the nurse.

Luke Bass (9)
Stanstead Primary School

SOMEWHERE IN OUR SCHOOL TODAY . . .

A group of children stupidly race to the line.
Half of Class 3 were busily bursting for the toilet.
Five crazy teachers were precariously hoping to be ducks.
Six of the teachers were playing a very rough game of basketball.
Mrs Booker was making hot cross buns while skilfully
writing maths puzzles on the board.
Miss Wilde was chewing gum while Class 4 were happily doing art.
Mr Gum was unfortunately cleaning up the boys toilets
because someone had pulled the pipes apart.
Twelve happy infants skilfully looking up a web page.

Rachel Reid (9)
Stanstead Primary School